FOR ORGANS, PIANOS & ELECTRONIC KEYBOARDS

107

THE BEST
PRAISE & WORSHIP SONGS EVER

PRAISE & Worship

ISBN 978-1-4234-6066-4

HAL•LEONARD®
CORPORATION

7777 W. BLUEMOUND RD. P.O. BOX 13819 MILWAUKEE, WI 53213

E-Z Play® Today Music Notation © 1975 by HAL LEONARD CORPORATION

E-Z PLAY and EASY ELECTRONIC KEYBOARD MUSIC are registered trademarks of HAL LEONARD CORPORATION.

Visit Hal Leonard Online at
www.halleonard.com

CONTENTS

Above All

Registration 1
Rhythm: Ballad or 8 Beat

Words and Music by Paul Baloche
and Lenny LeBlanc

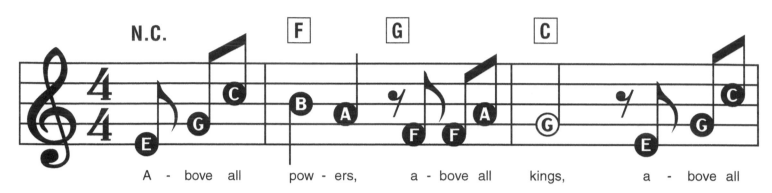

A - bove all pow - ers, a - bove all kings, a - bove all

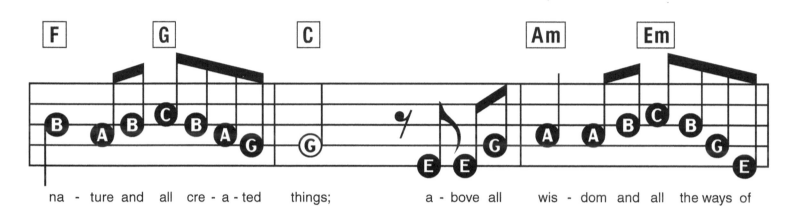

na - ture and all cre - a - ted things; a - bove all wis - dom and all the ways of

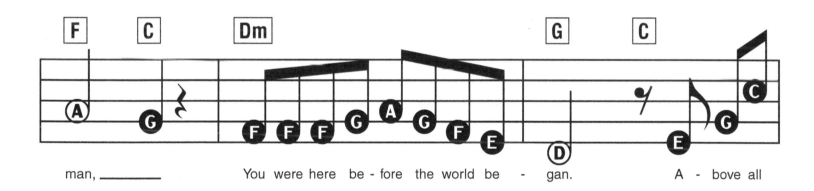

man, _____ You were here be - fore the world be - gan. A - bove all

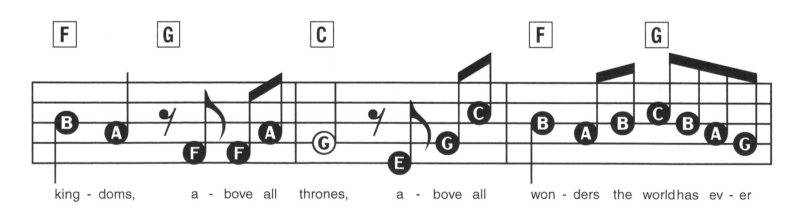

king - doms, a - bove all thrones, a - bove all won - ders the world has ev - er

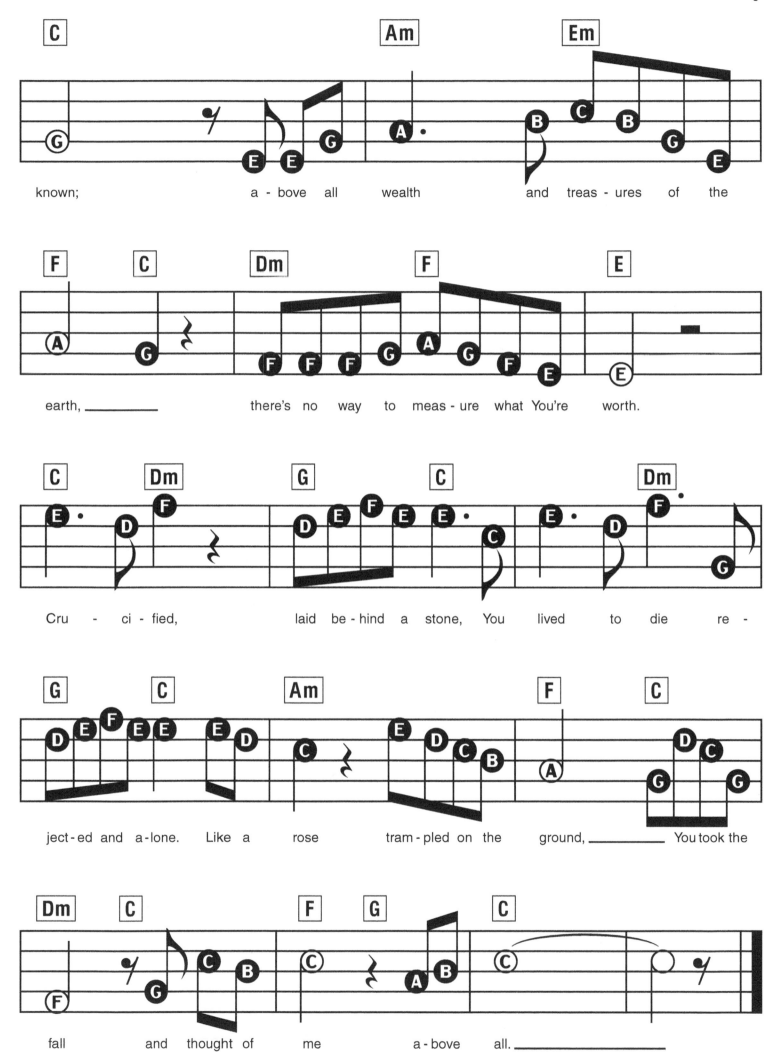

Agnus Dei

Registration 1
Rhythm: Ballad or 8 Beat

Words and Music by
Michael W. Smith

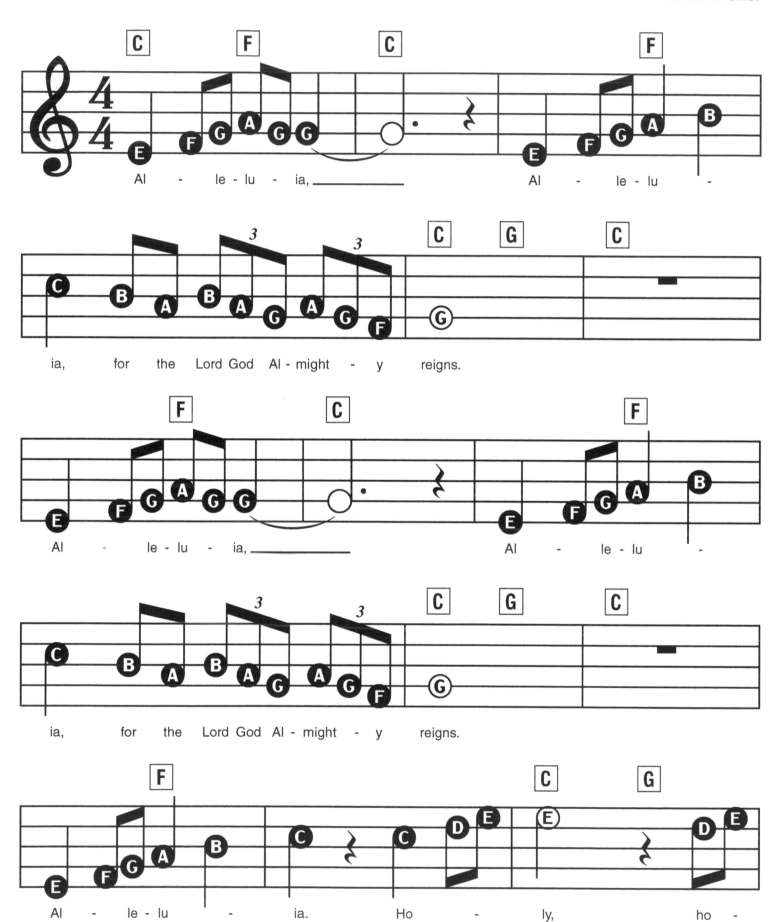

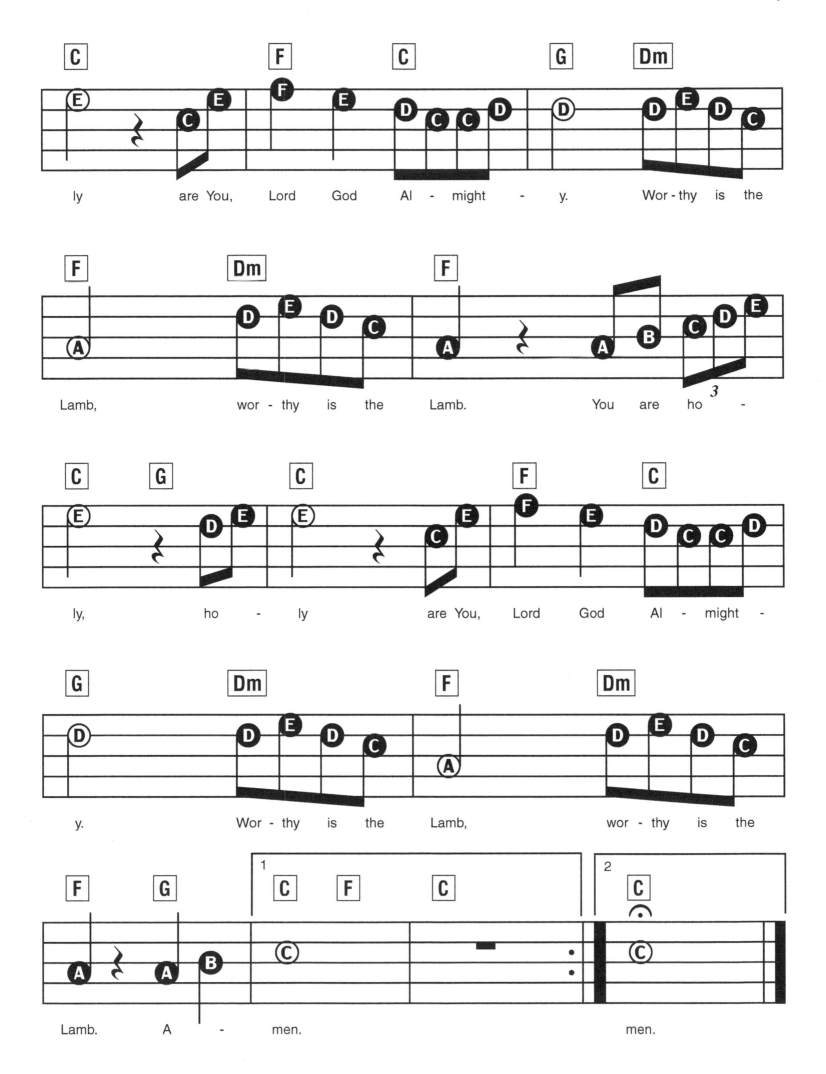

7

Ancient of Days

Registration 2
Rhythm: Rock or March

Words and Music by Gary Sadler
and Jamie Harvill

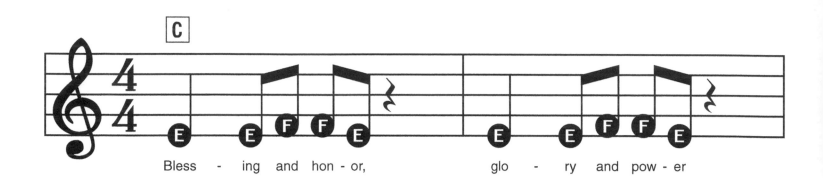

Bless - ing and hon - or, glo - ry and pow - er

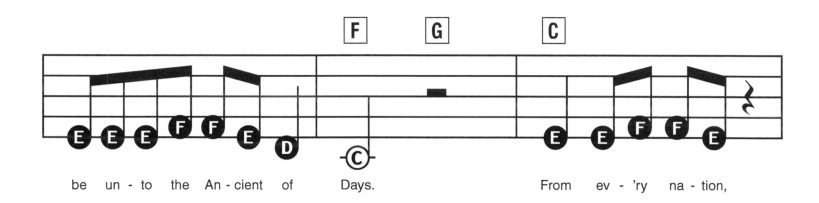

be un - to the An - cient of Days. From ev - 'ry na - tion,

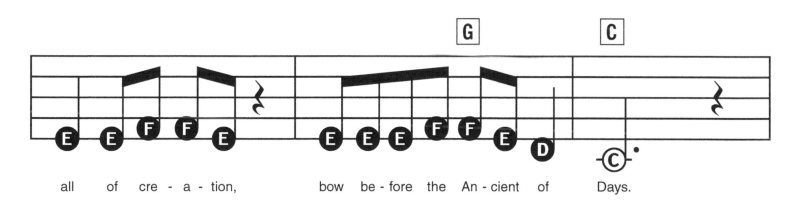

all of cre - a - tion, bow be - fore the An - cient of Days.

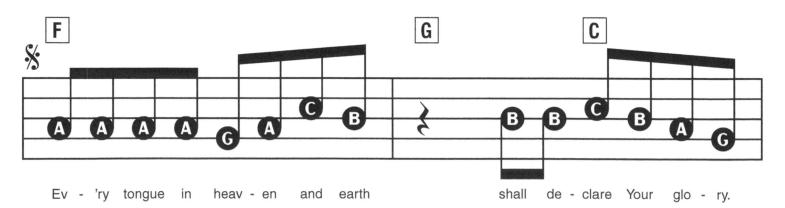

Ev - 'ry tongue in heav - en and earth shall de - clare Your glo - ry.

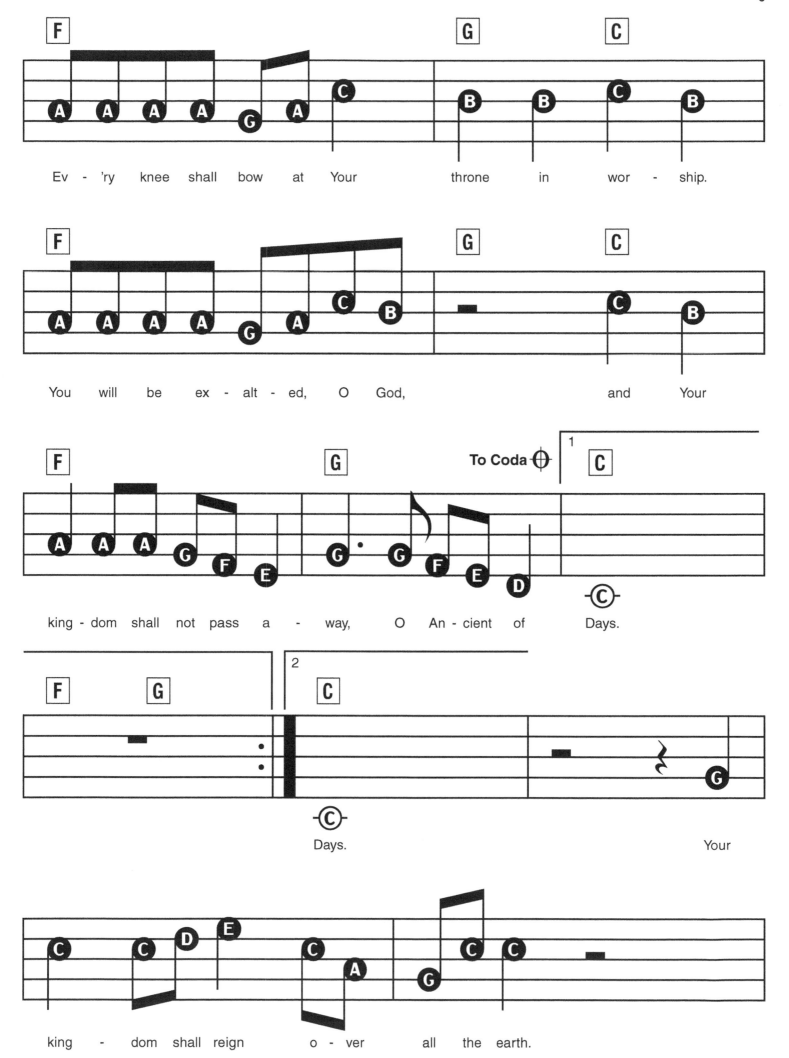

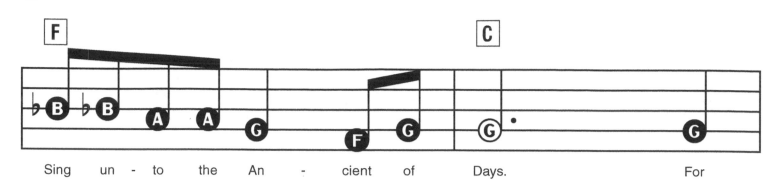

Sing un - to the An - cient of Days. For

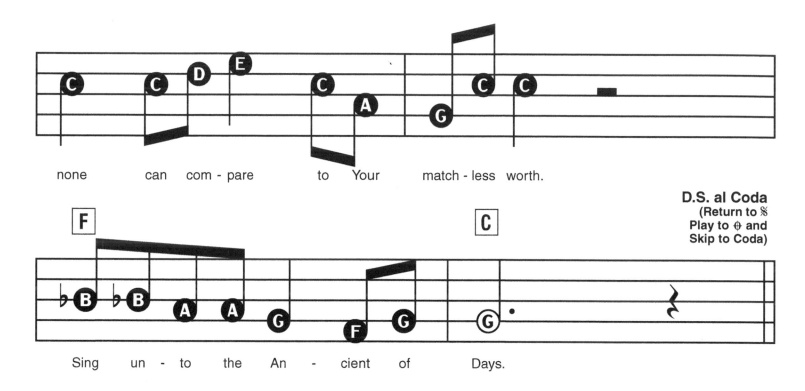

none can com - pare to Your match - less worth.

D.S. al Coda
(Return to 𝄋
Play to ⊕ and
Skip to Coda)

Sing un - to the An - cient of Days.

CODA

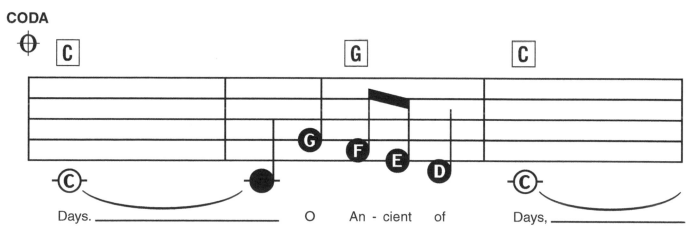

Days. _____ O An - cient of Days, _____

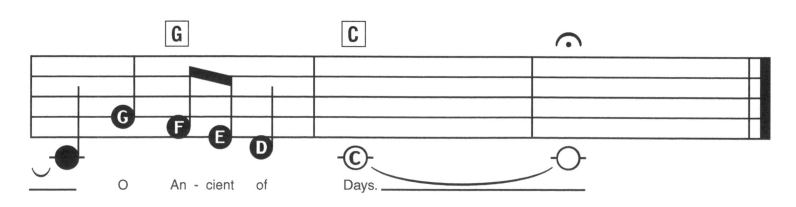

O An - cient of Days. _____

Blessed Be Your Name

Registration 8
Rhythm: 8 Beat or Rock

Words and Music by Matt Redman
and Beth Redman

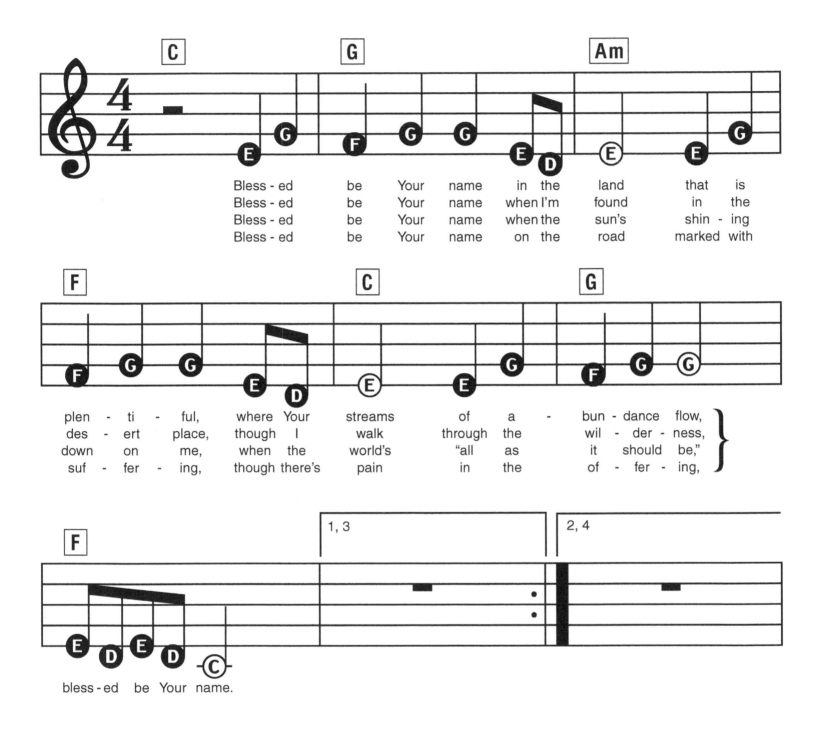

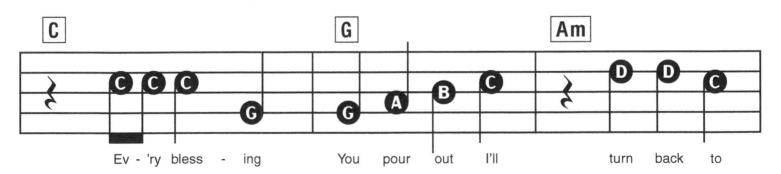

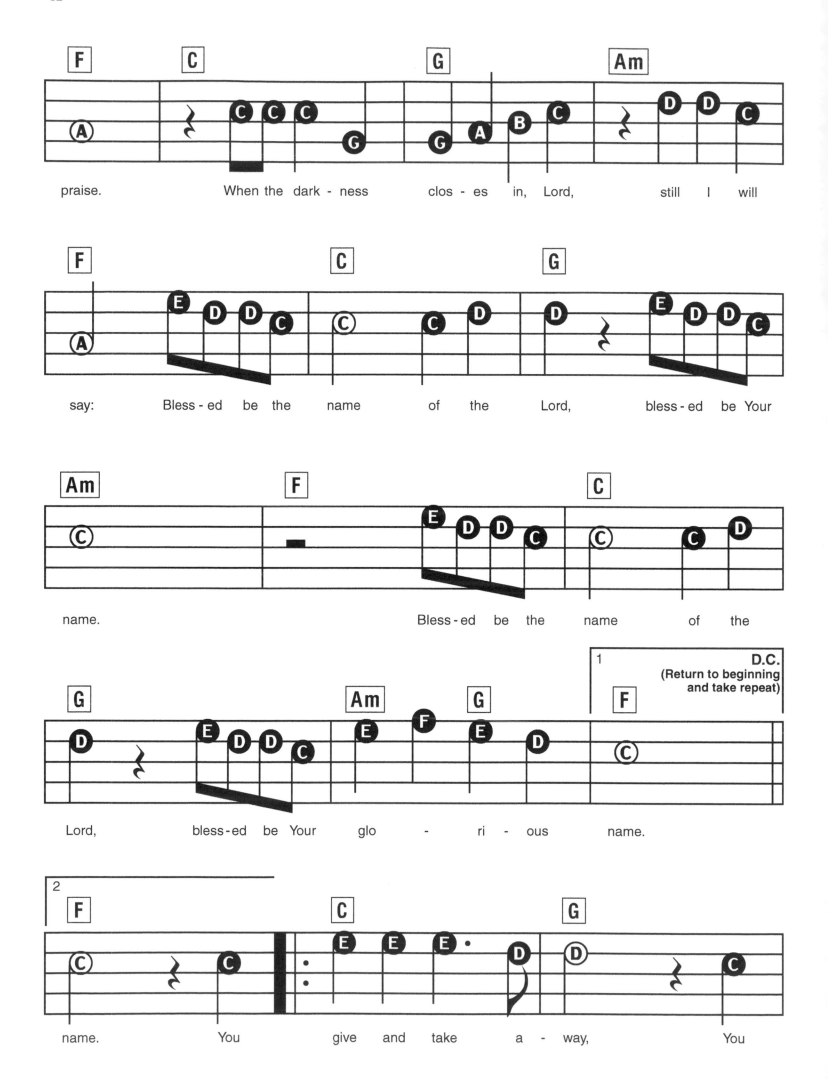

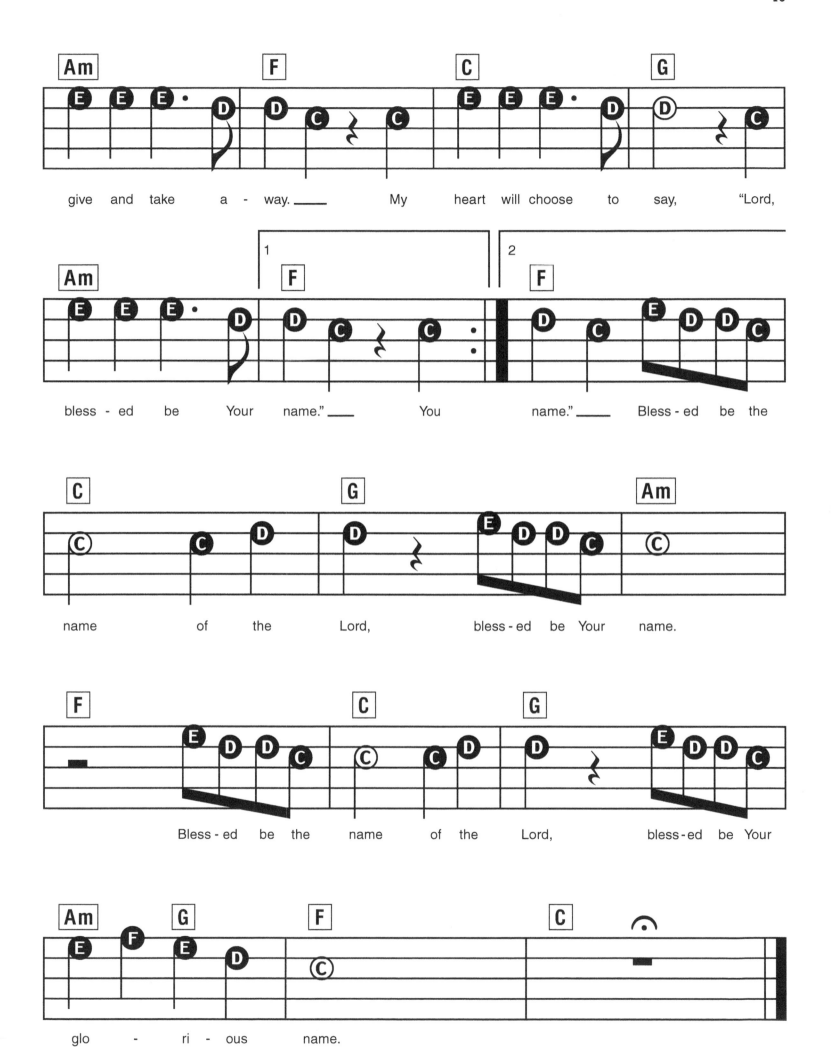

As the Deer

Registration 1
Rhythm: Ballad or 8 Beat

Words and Music by
Martin Nystrom

Awesome God

Registration 7
Rhythm: 16 Beat or Pop

Words and Music by
Rich Mullins

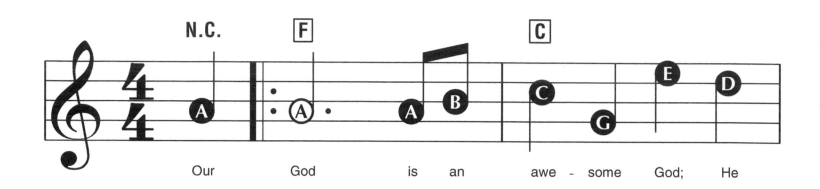

Our God is an awe - some God; He

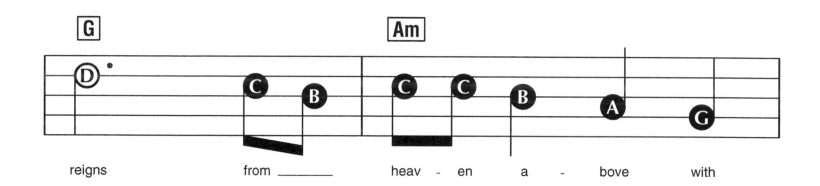

reigns from _____ heav - en a - bove with

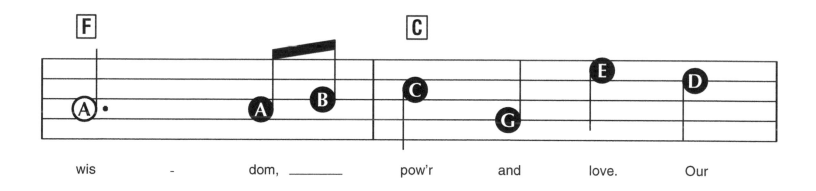

wis - dom, _____ pow'r and love. Our

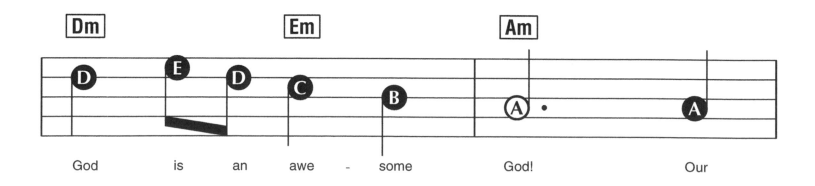

God is an awe - some God! Our

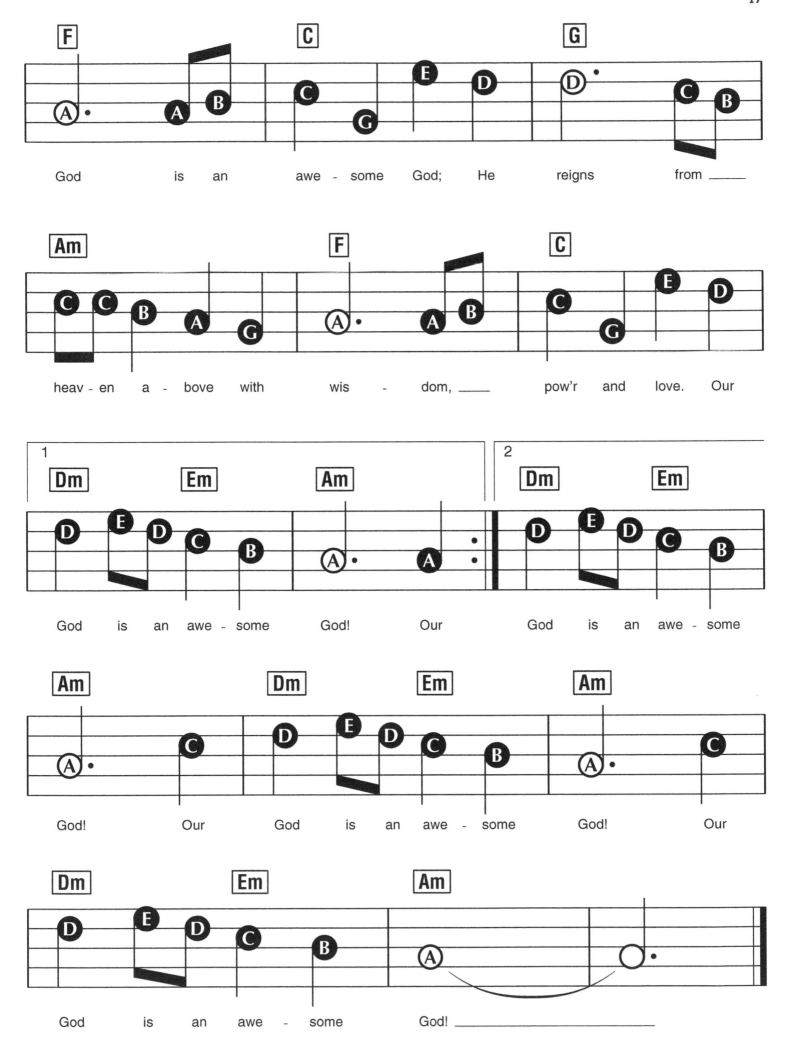

Be Unto Your Name

Registration 1
Rhythm: Waltz

Words and Music by Lynn DeShazo
and Gary Sadler

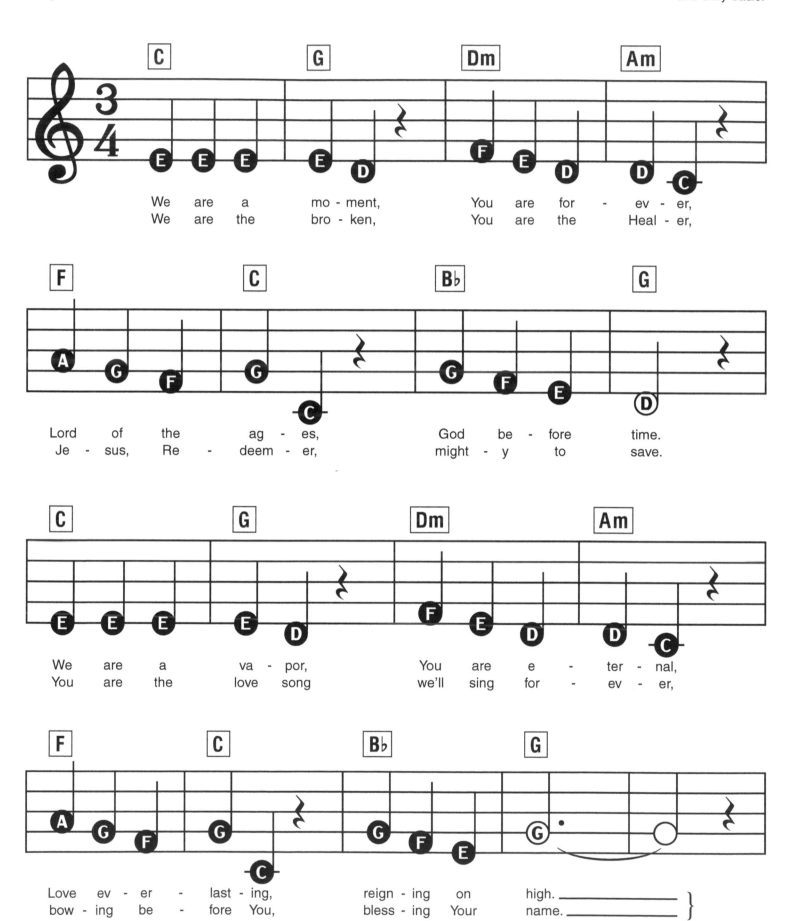

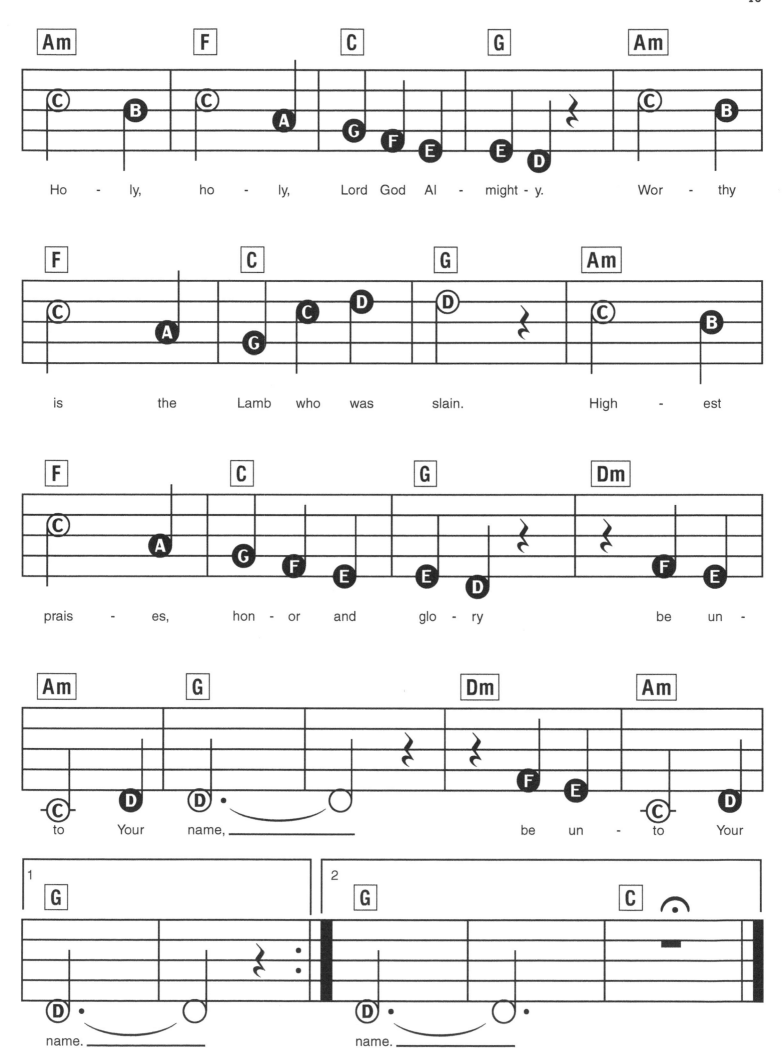

Better Is One Day

Registration 2
Rhythm: 8 Beat or Pop

Words and Music by
Matt Redman

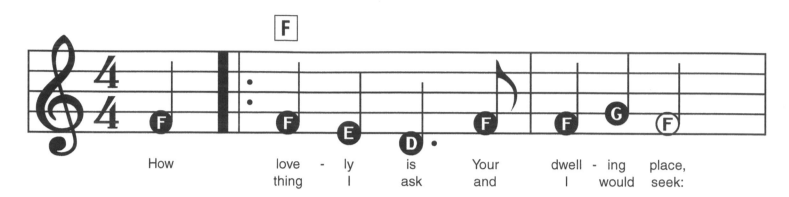

How   love - ly   is   Your   dwell - ing   place,
thing   I   ask   and   I   would seek:

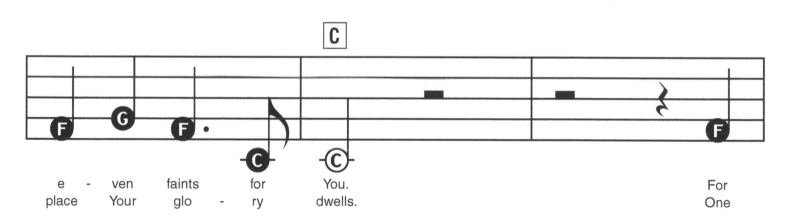

O   Lord   Al - might - y,   for   my   soul   longs and
to   see   Your beau - ty,   to   find   You   in   the

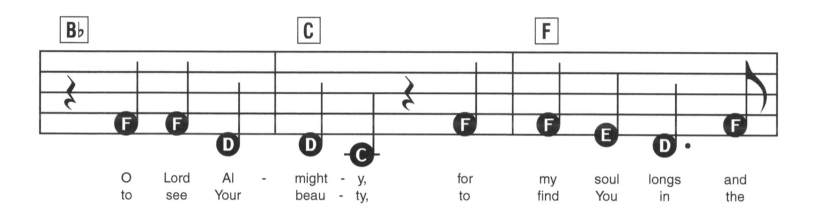

e - ven   faints   for   You.   For
place Your glo - ry   dwells.   One

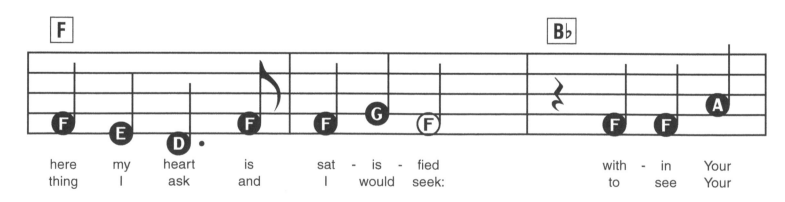

here   my   heart   is   sat - is - fied   with - in   Your
thing   I   ask   and   I   would seek: to   see   Your

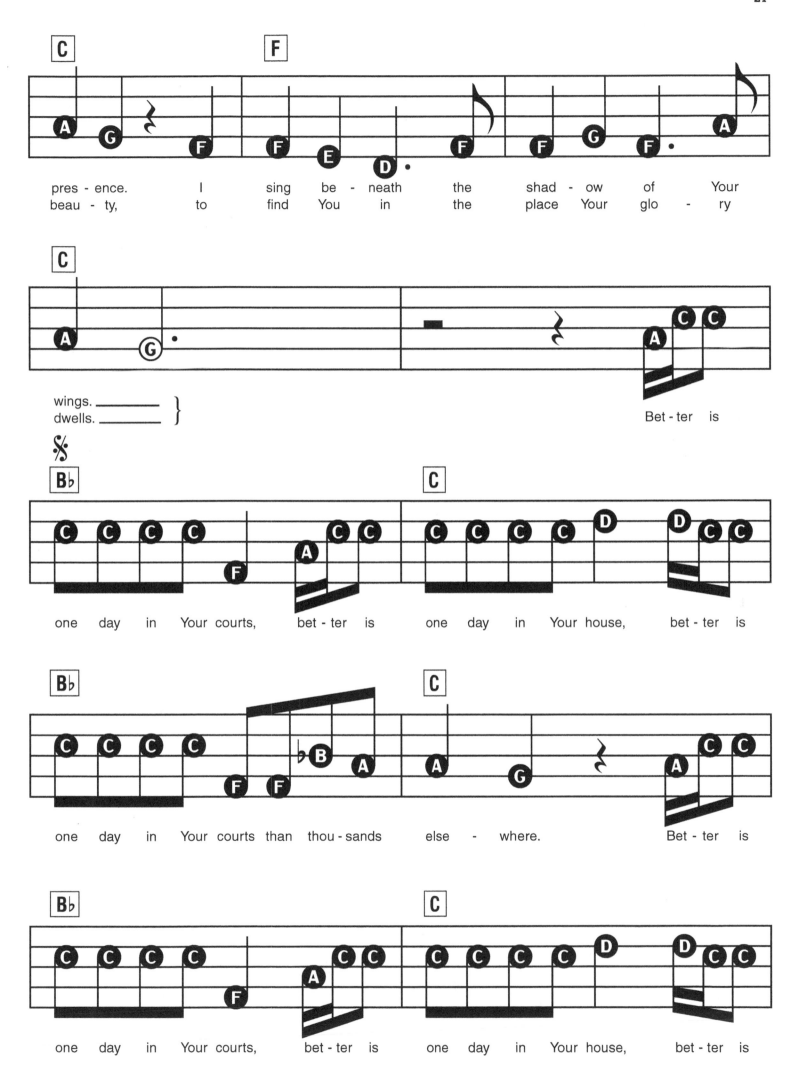

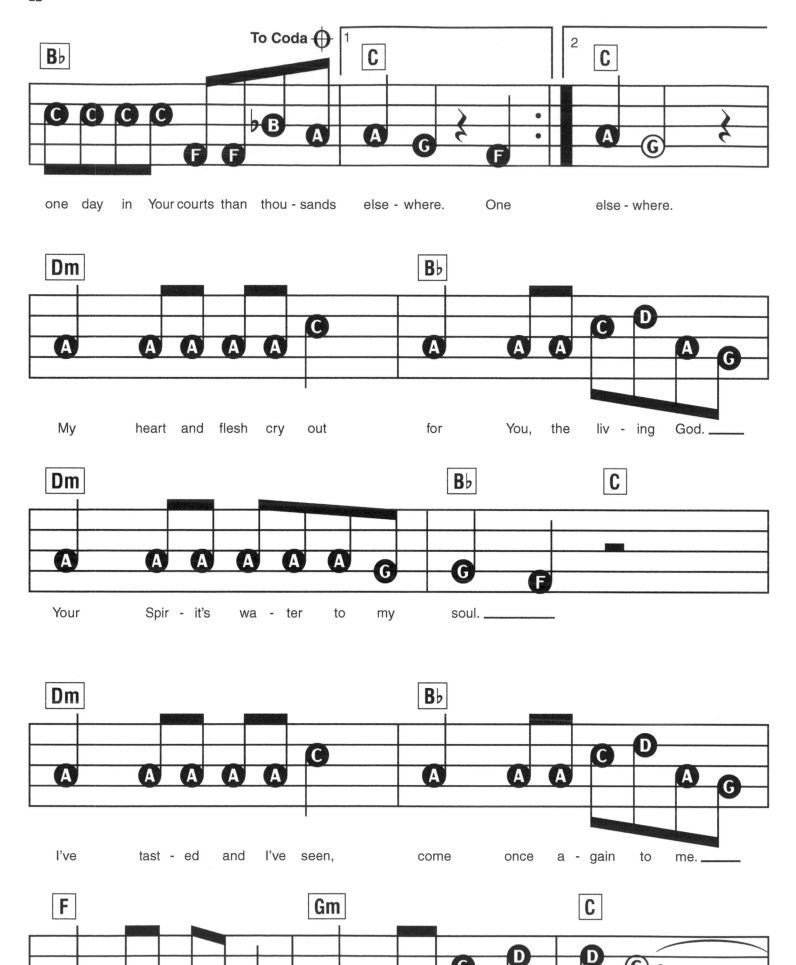

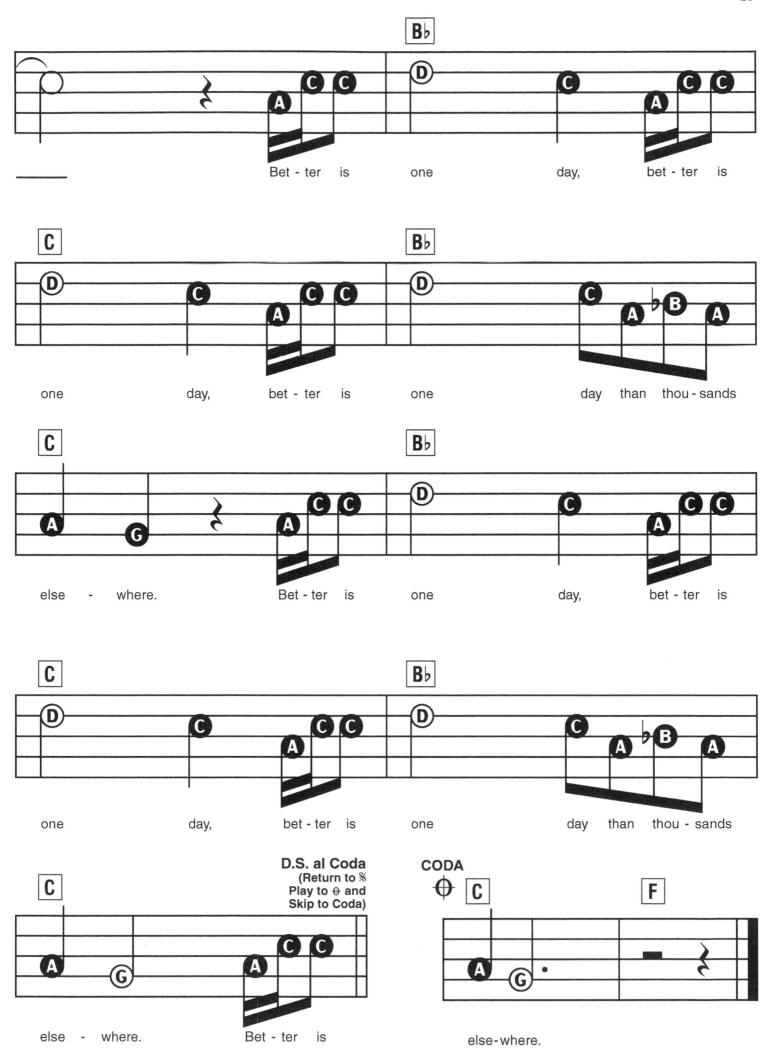

Breathe

Registration 1
Rhythm: Ballad or 8 Beat

Words and Music by
Marie Barnett

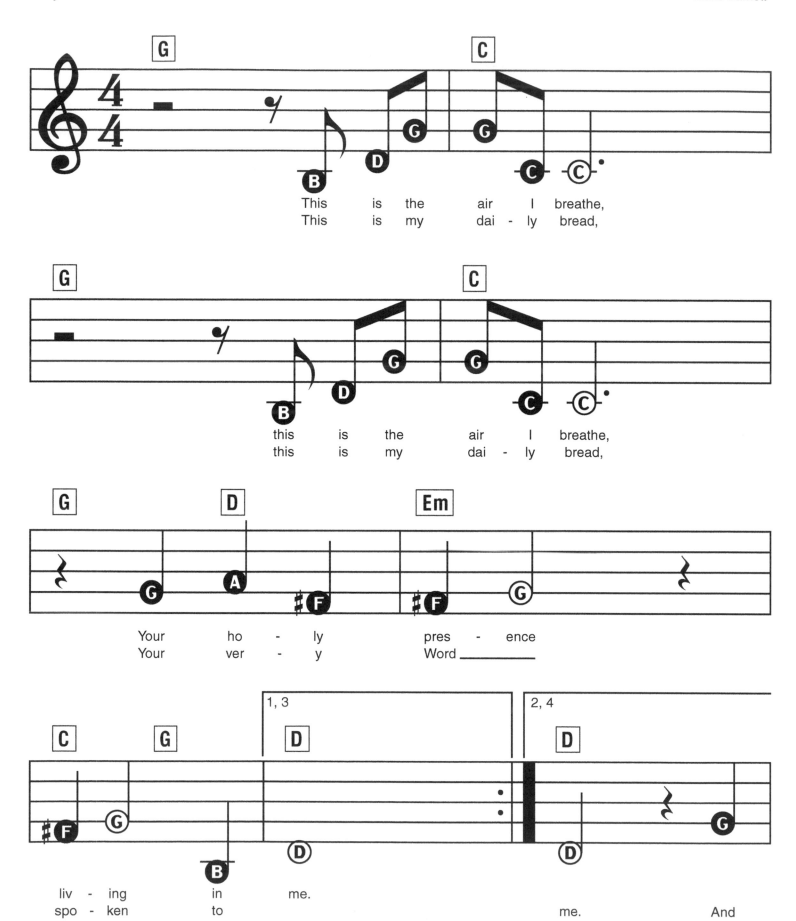

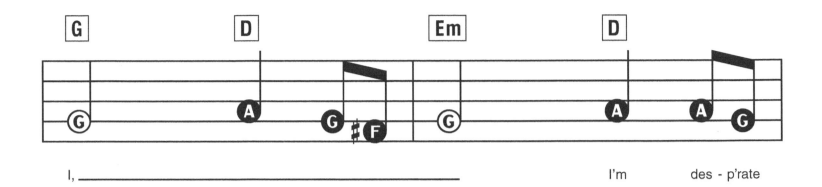

I, _____ I'm des - p'rate

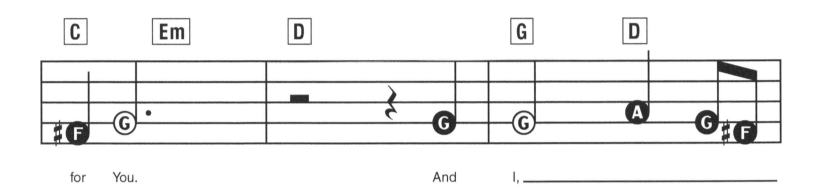

for You. And I, _____

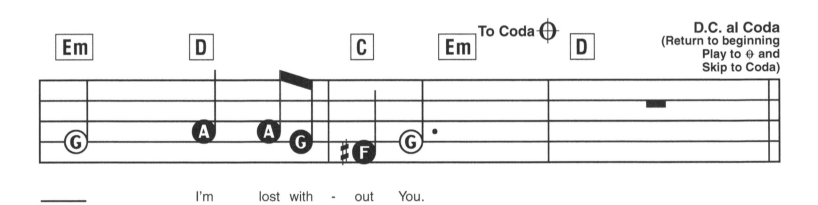

_____ I'm lost with - out You.

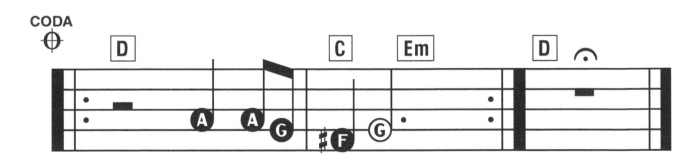

I'm lost with - out You.

Come Into His Presence

Registration 2
Rhythm: 8 Beat or Rock

Words and Music by
Lynn Baird

C

G G G A G F E F

Come in-to His pres-ence with thanks - giv-ing in your heart and give Him

Dm   **G**   **C**

F E D A G G G G A G F E F

praise,   and give Him praise.   Come in-to His pres-ence with thanks -

Dm   **G**

G G G A G F E G F E D A G G

giv-ing in your heart, your voic - es raise,   your voic - es raise.   Give

F   **E7 E**   **Am**   **Fm**

A A A B B B C C B C D E D C D

glo - ry and hon - or and pow - er un - to Him, _____

C   **Am**   **Dm**   **G7 G**   **C**   **F**   **C**

E D C C D D C B C C

Je - sus, the name a - bove all names. _____

Celebrate Jesus

Registration 7
Rhythm: Rock or 8 Beat

Words and Music by
Gary Oliver

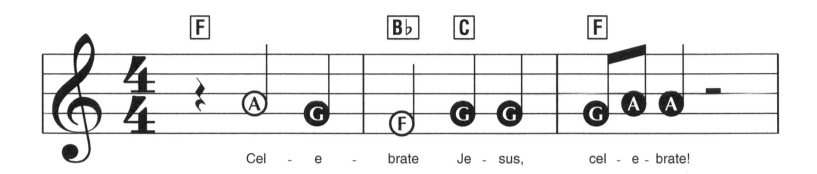

Cel - e - brate Je - sus, cel - e - brate!

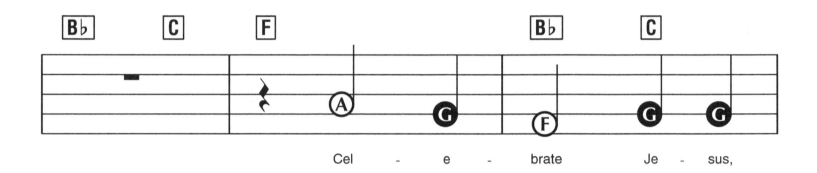

Cel - e - brate Je - sus,

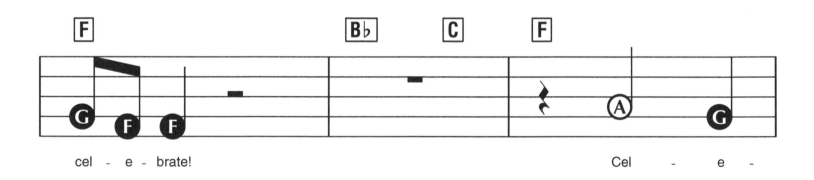

cel - e - brate! Cel - e -

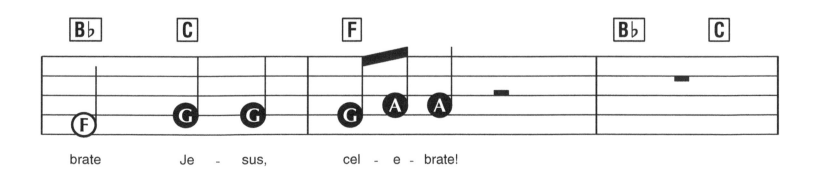

brate Je - sus, cel - e - brate!

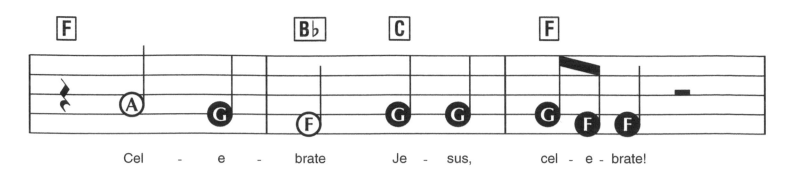

Cel - e - brate Je - sus, cel - e - brate!

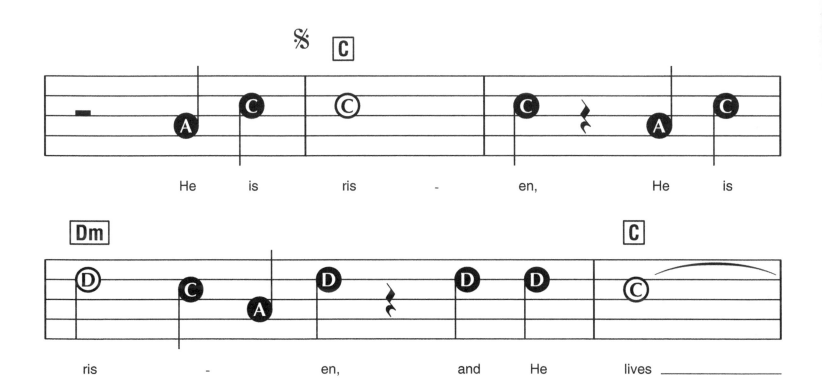

He is ris - en, He is

ris - en, and He lives

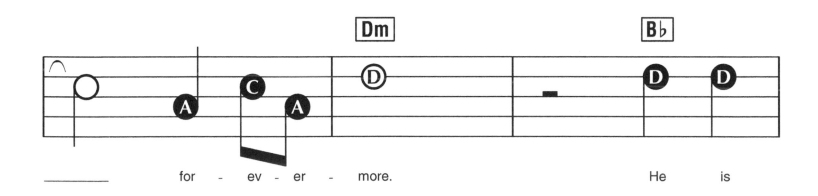

_____ for - ev - er - more. He is

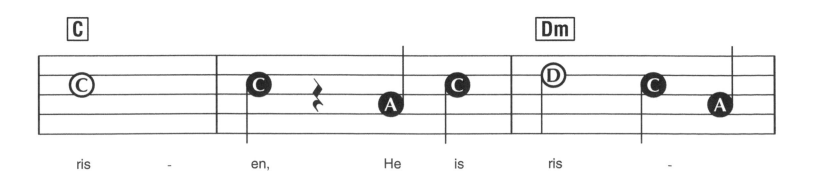

ris - en, He is ris -

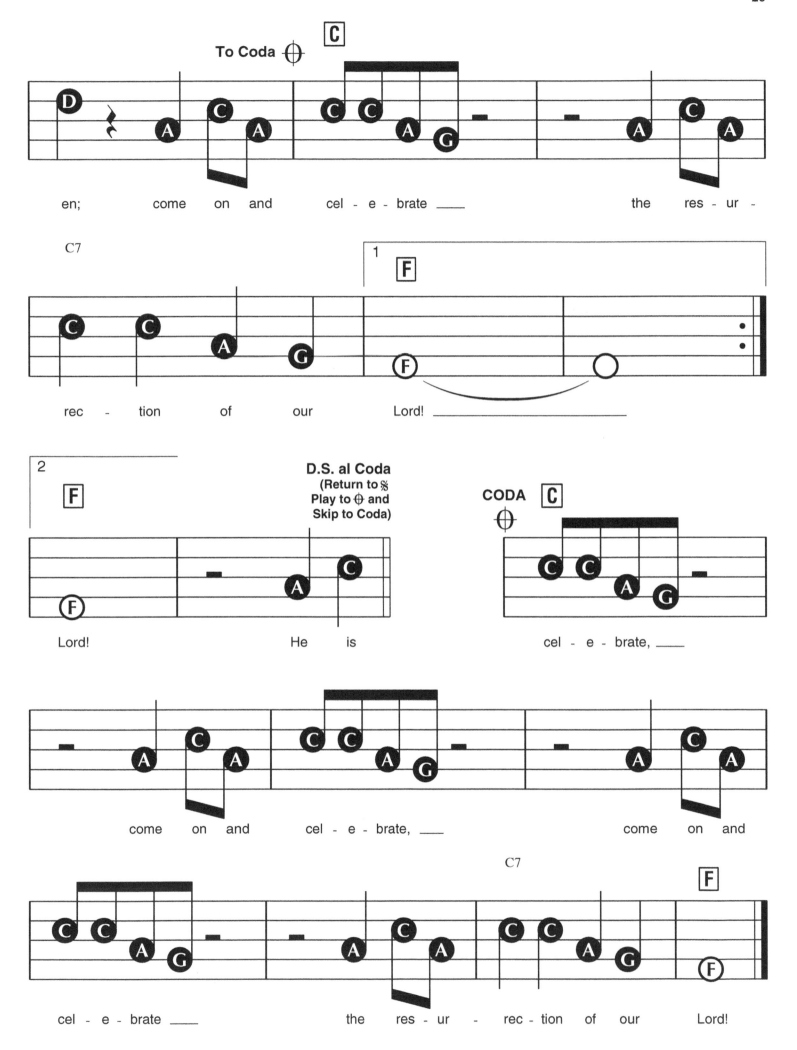

Change My Heart Oh God

Registration 3
Rhythm: Ballad or 8 Beat

Words and Music by
Eddie Espinosa

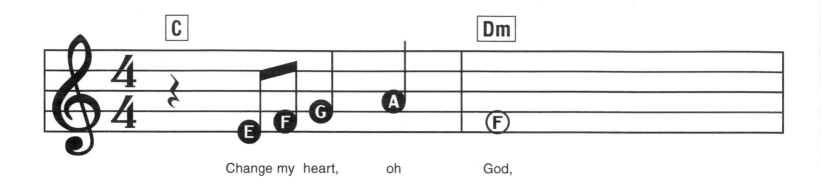

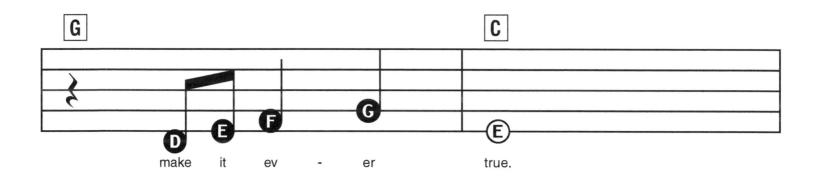

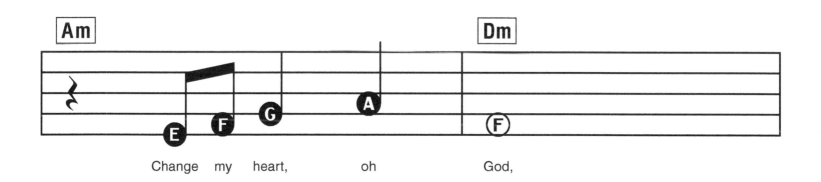

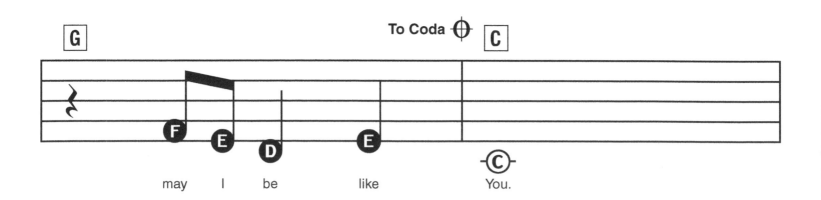

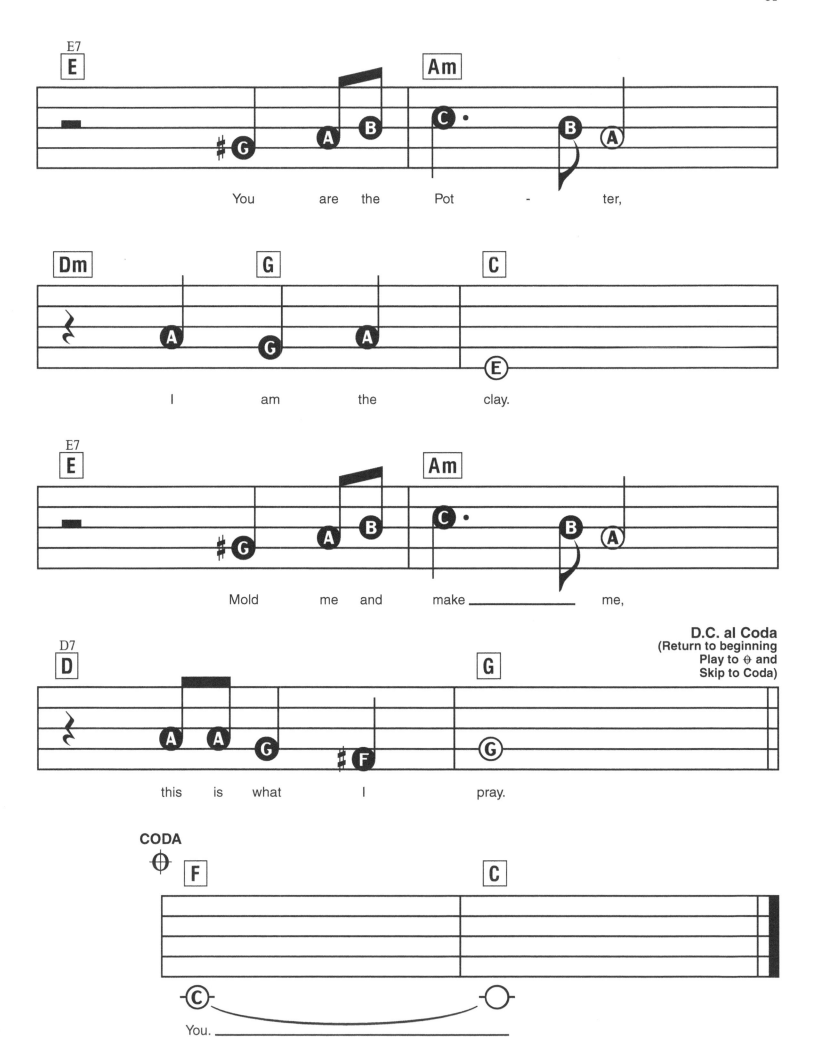

Come, Now Is the Time to Worship

Registration 7
Rhythm: 8 Beat or Rock

Words and Music by
Brian Doerksen

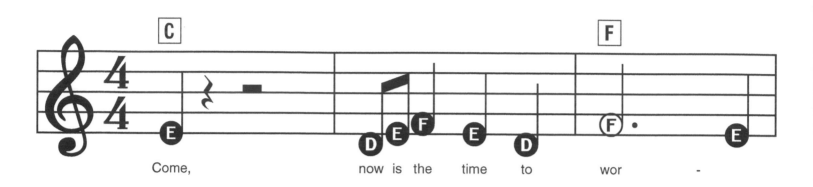

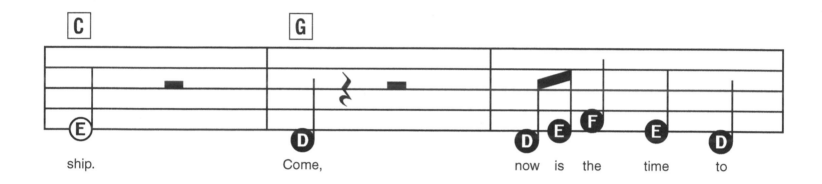

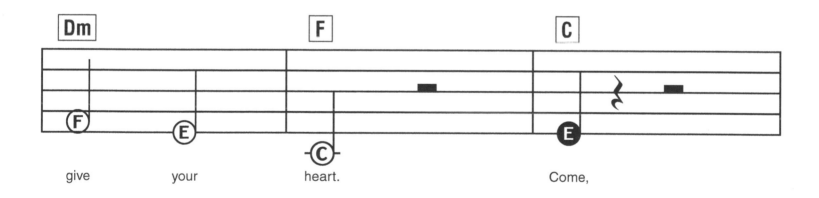

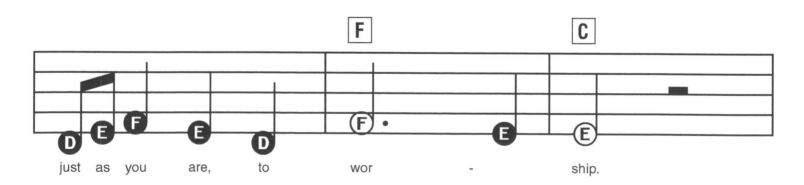

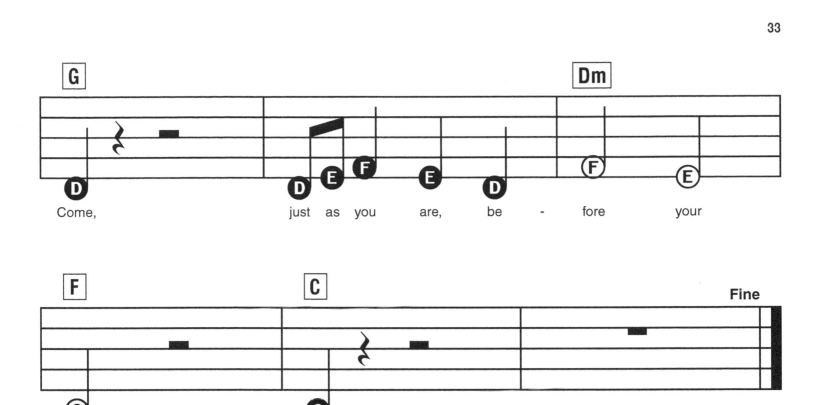

Come, just as you are, be - fore your

God. Come.

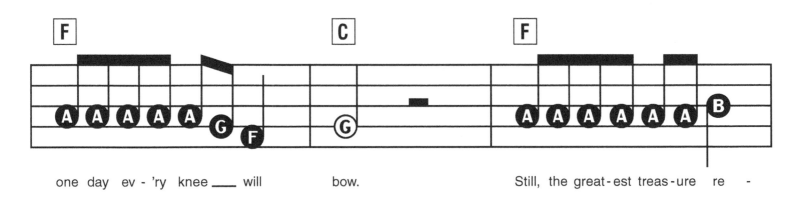

One day ev - 'ry tongue will con - fess You are God,

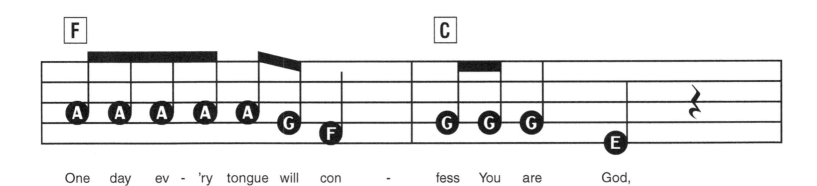

one day ev - 'ry knee ___ will bow. Still, the great - est treas - ure re -

D.C. al Fine
(Return to beginning and
Play to Fine)

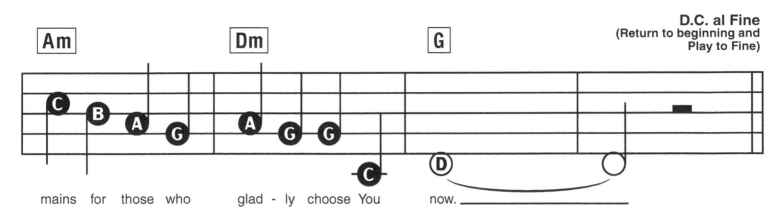

mains for those who glad - ly choose You now. ___

Create in Me a Clean Heart

Registration 8
Rhythm: Ballad

Words and Music by
Keith Green

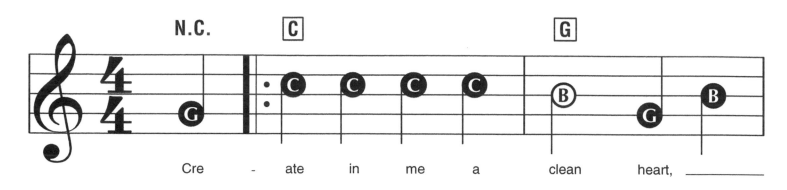

Cre - ate in me a clean heart, _____

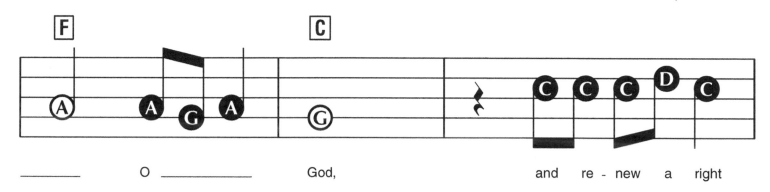

_____ O _____ God, and re-new a right

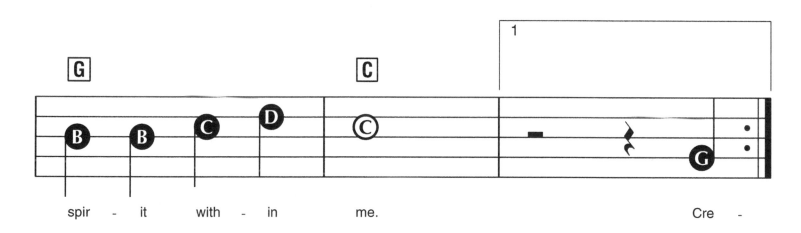

spir - it with - in me. Cre -

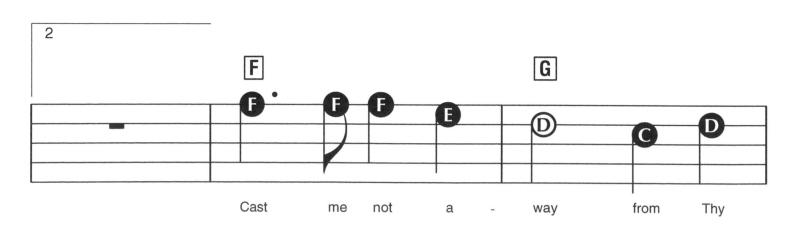

Cast me not a - way from Thy

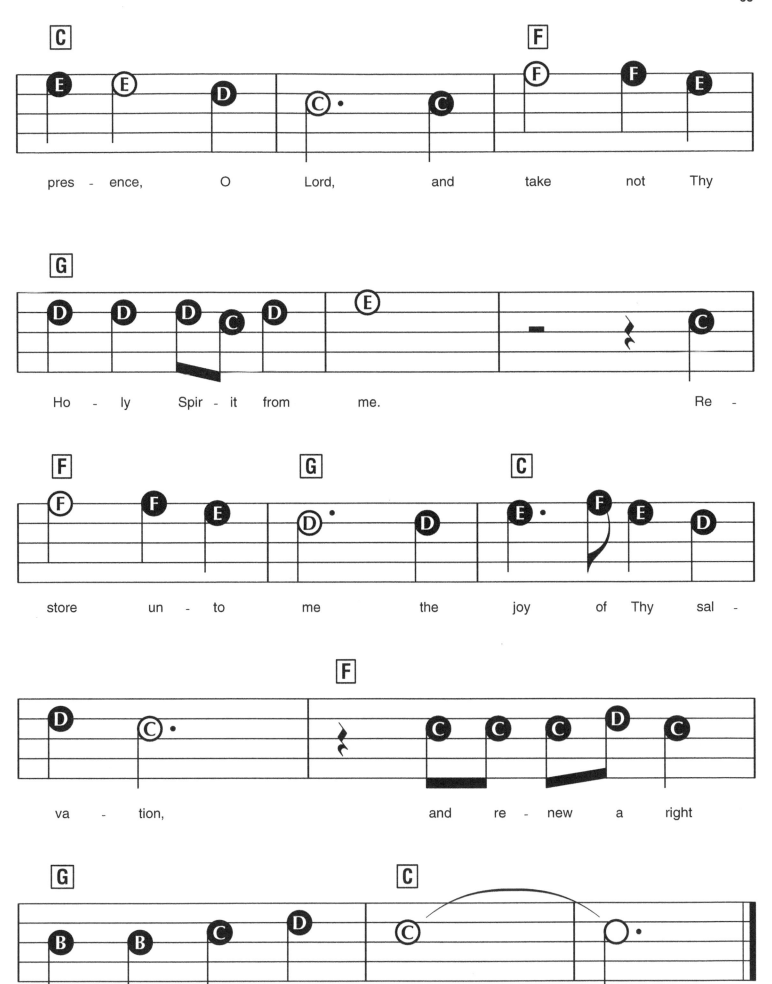

Days of Elijah

Registration 7
Rhythm: Pop or March

Words and Music by
Robin Mark

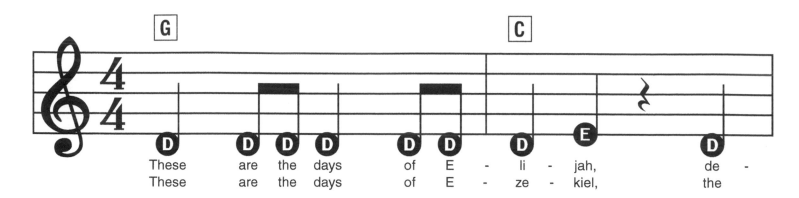

These are the days of E - li - jah, de -
These are the days of E - ze - kiel, the

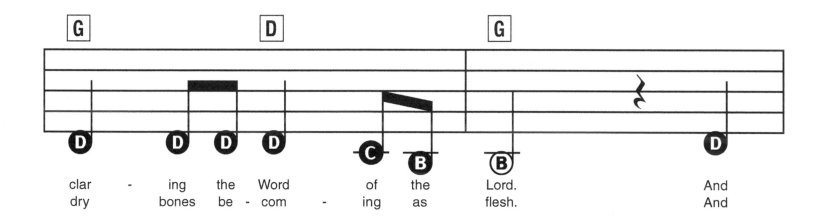

clar - ing the Word of the Lord. And
dry bones be - com - ing as flesh. And

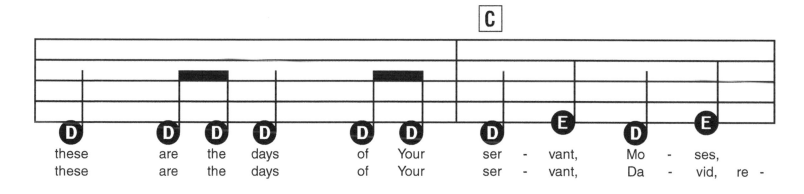

these are the days of Your ser - vant, Mo - ses,
these are the days of Your ser - vant, Da - vid, re -

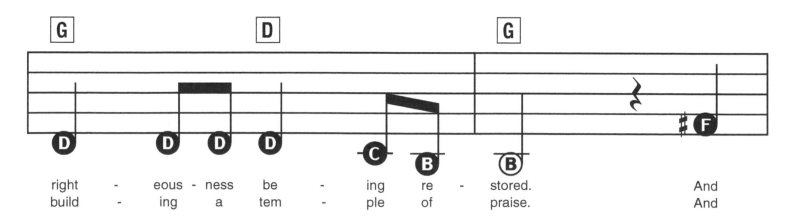

right - eous - ness be - ing re - stored. And
build - ing a tem - ple of praise. And

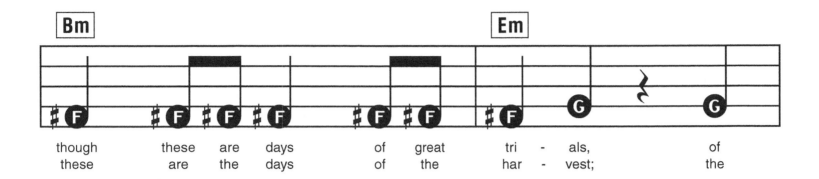

though these are days of great tri - als, of
these are the days of the har - vest; the

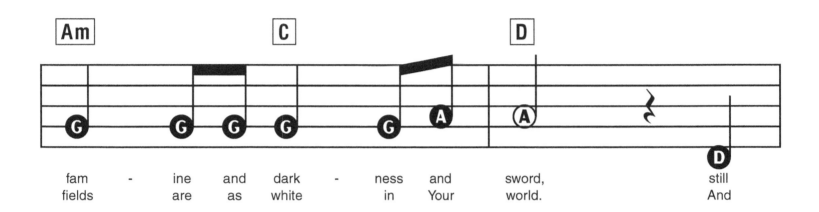

fam - ine and dark - ness and sword, still
fields are as white in Your world. And

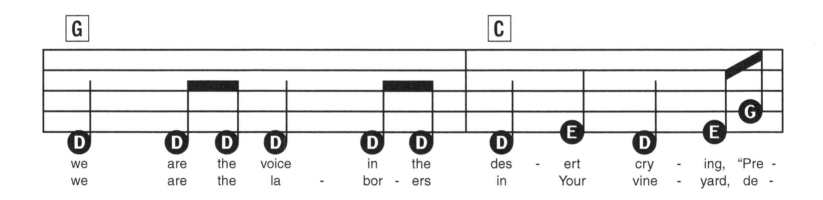

we are the voice in the des - ert cry - ing, "Pre -
we are the la - bor - ers in Your vine - yard, de -

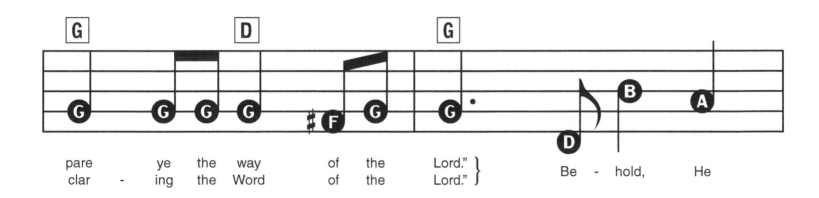

pare ye the way of the Lord." Be - hold, He
clar - ing the Word of the Lord."

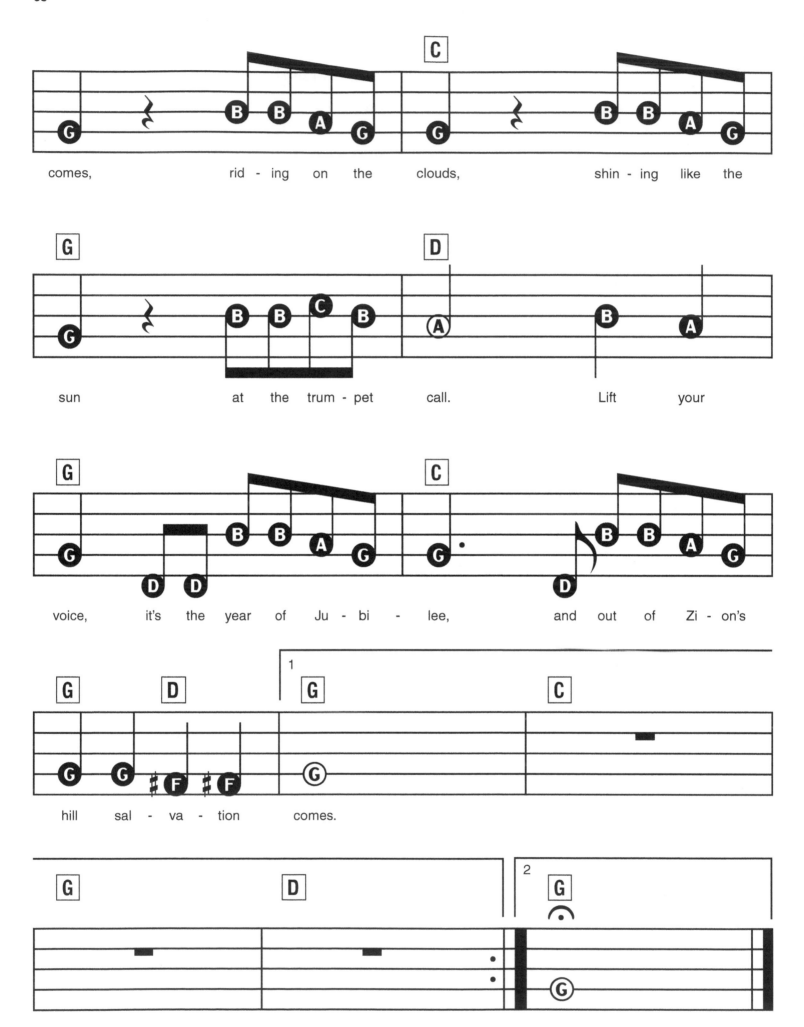

Give Thanks

Registration 1
Rhythm: Ballad

Words and Music by
Henry Smith

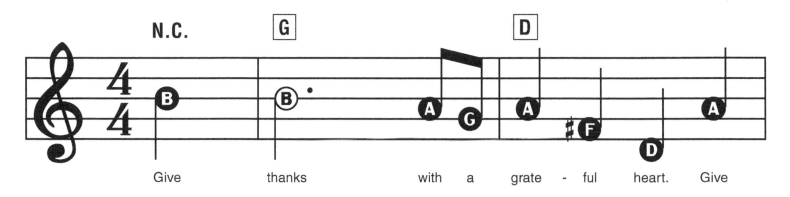

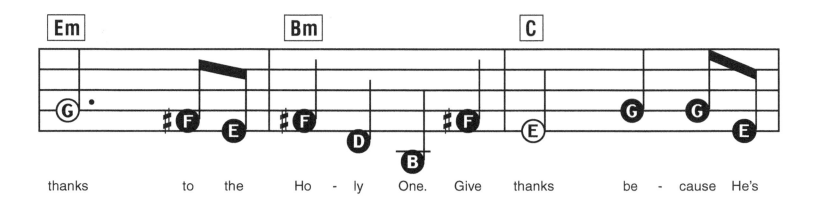

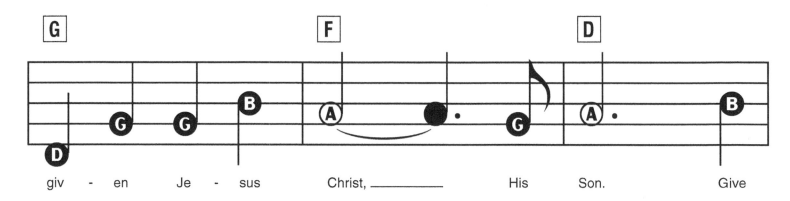

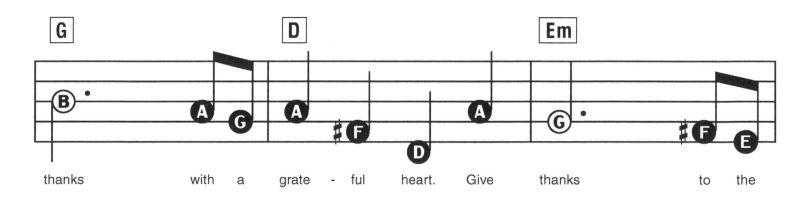

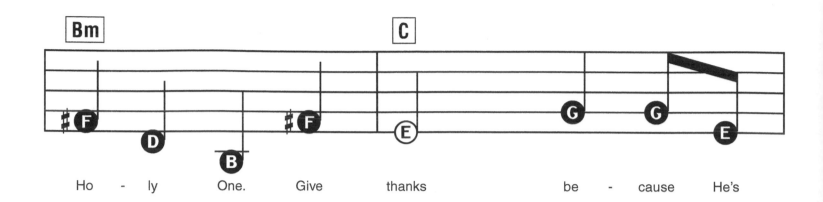

Ho - ly One. Give thanks be - cause He's

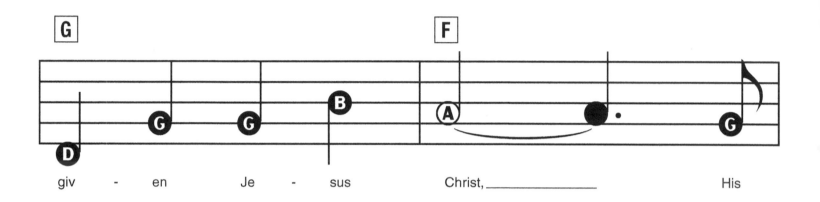

giv - en Je - sus Christ, _____ His

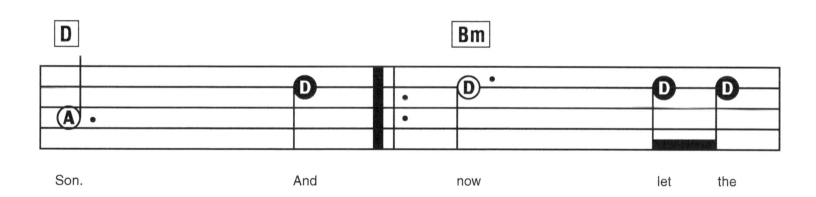

Son. And now let the

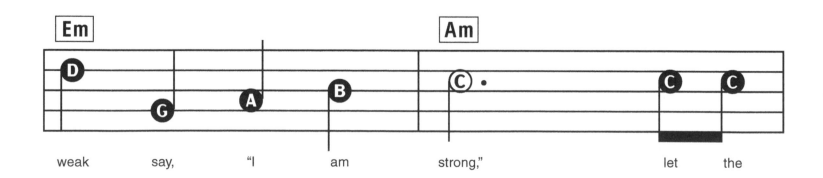

weak say, "I am strong," let the

41

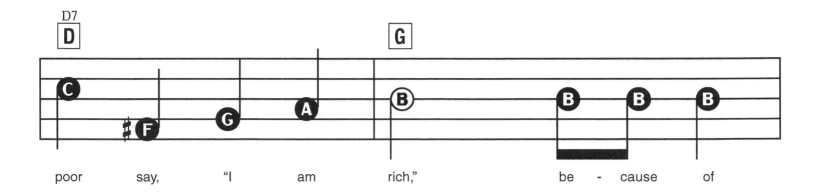

poor say, "I am rich," be - cause of

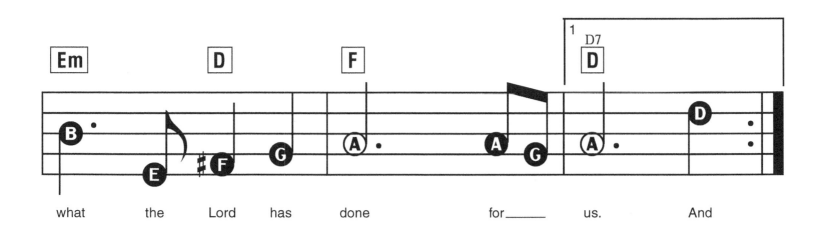

what the Lord has done for us. And

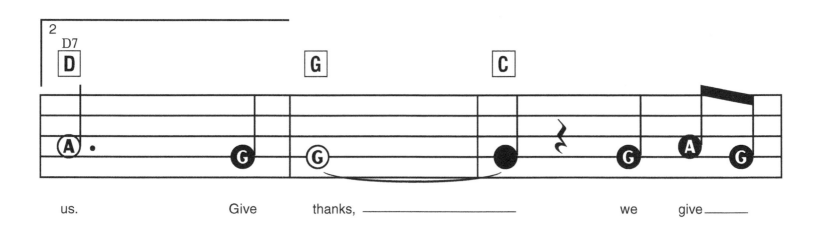

us. Give thanks, we give

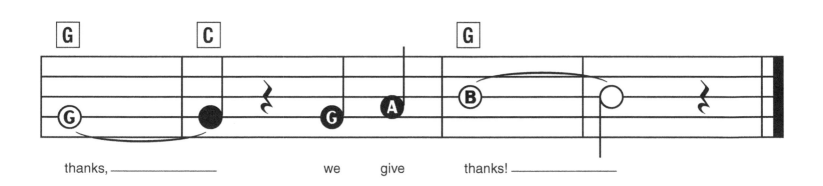

thanks, we give thanks!

Draw Me Close

Registration 1
Rhythm: Ballad or 8 Beat

Words and Music by
Kelly Carpenter

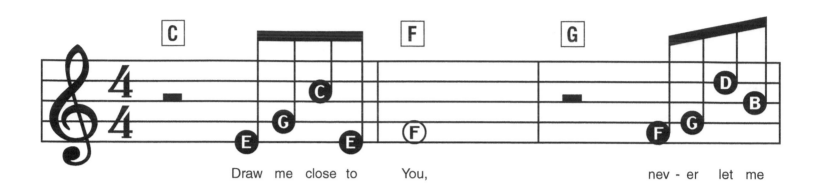

Draw me close to You, nev - er let me

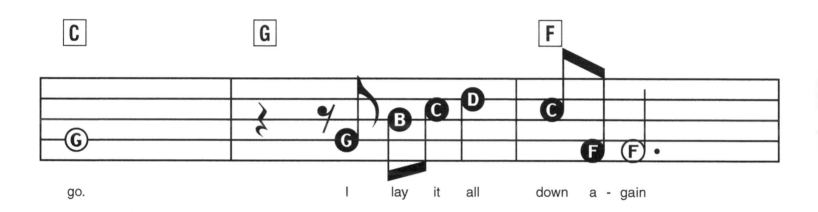

go. I lay it all down a - gain

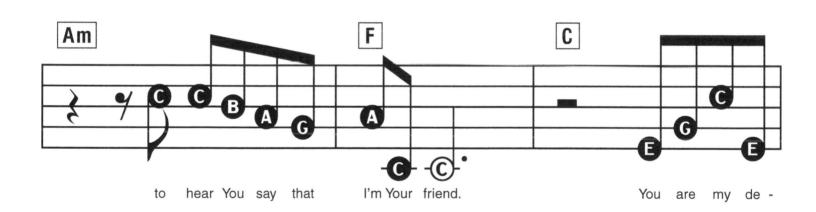

to hear You say that I'm Your friend. You are my de -

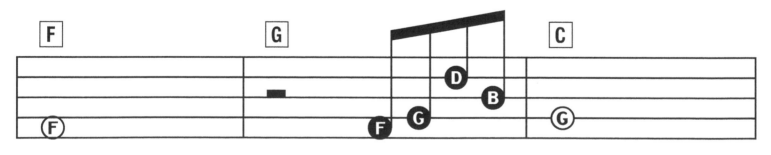

sire, no one else will do.

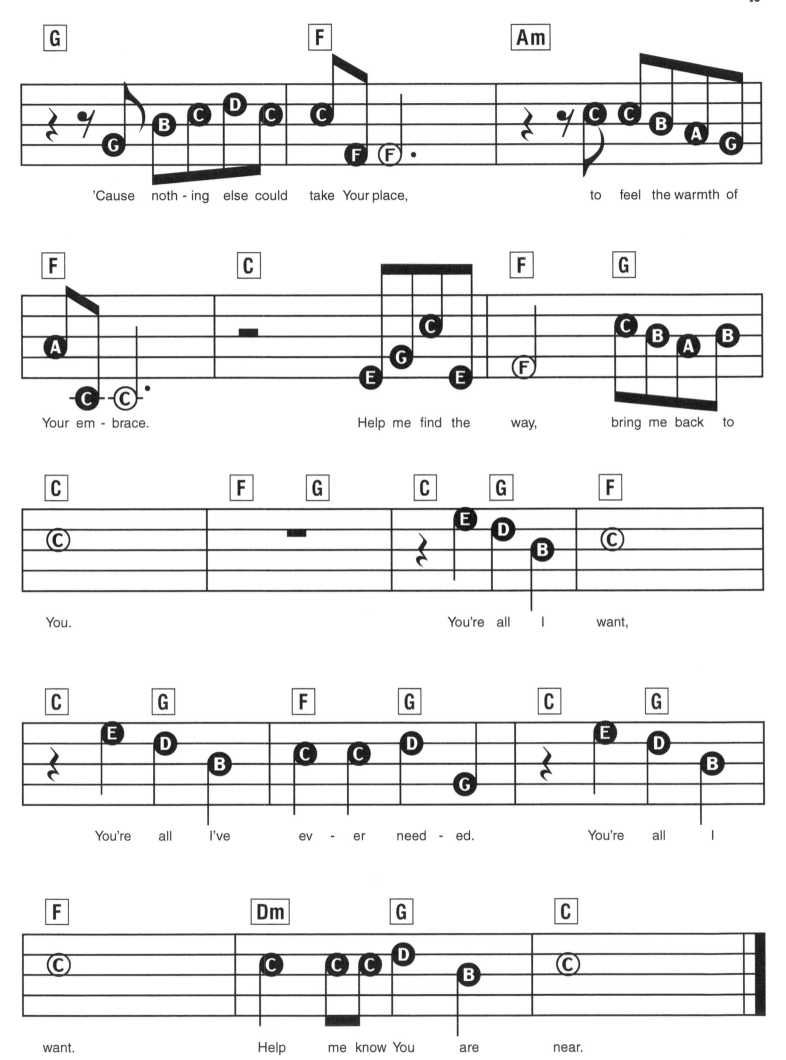

Enough

Registration 4
Rhythm: 8 Beat or Pop

Words and Music by Chris Tomlin
and Louie Giglio

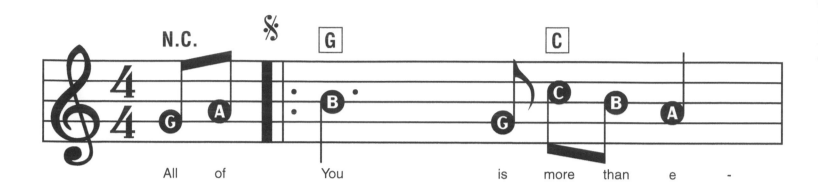

All of You is more than e -

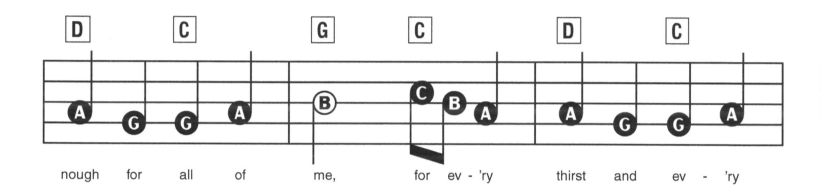

nough for all of me, for ev - 'ry thirst and ev - 'ry

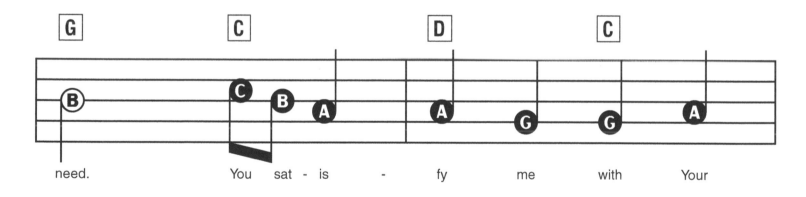

need. You sat - is - fy me with Your

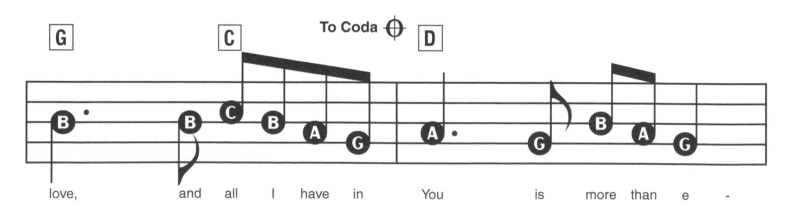

love, and all I have in You is more than e -

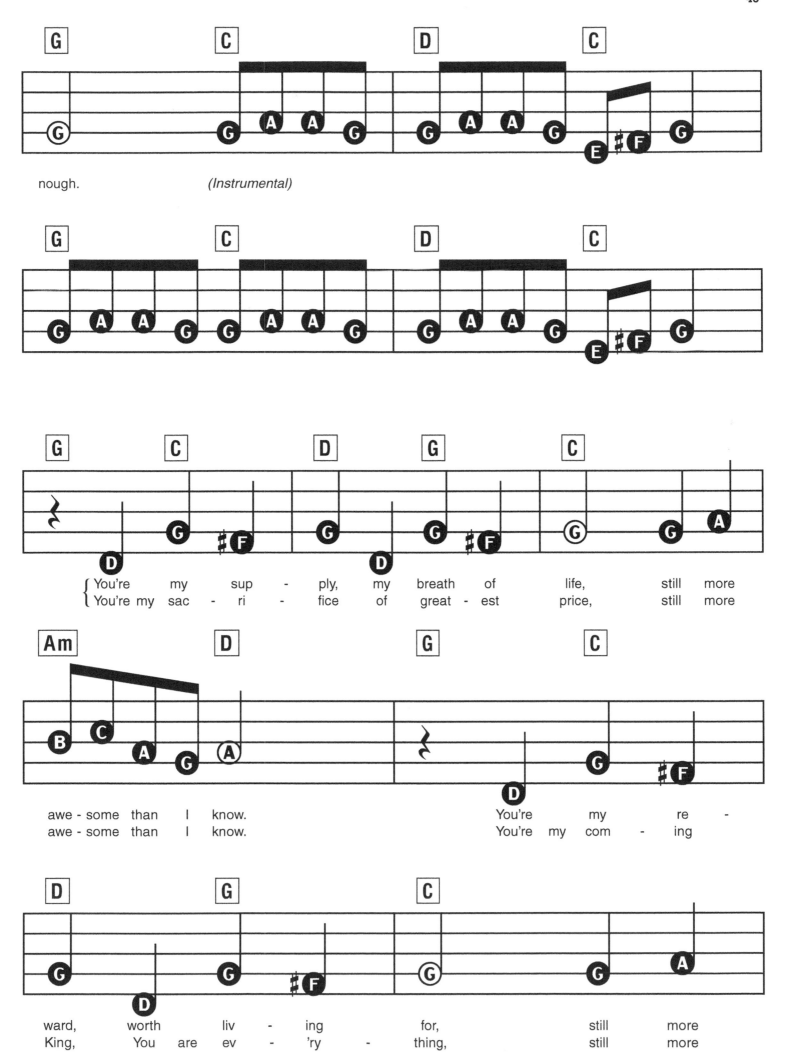

46

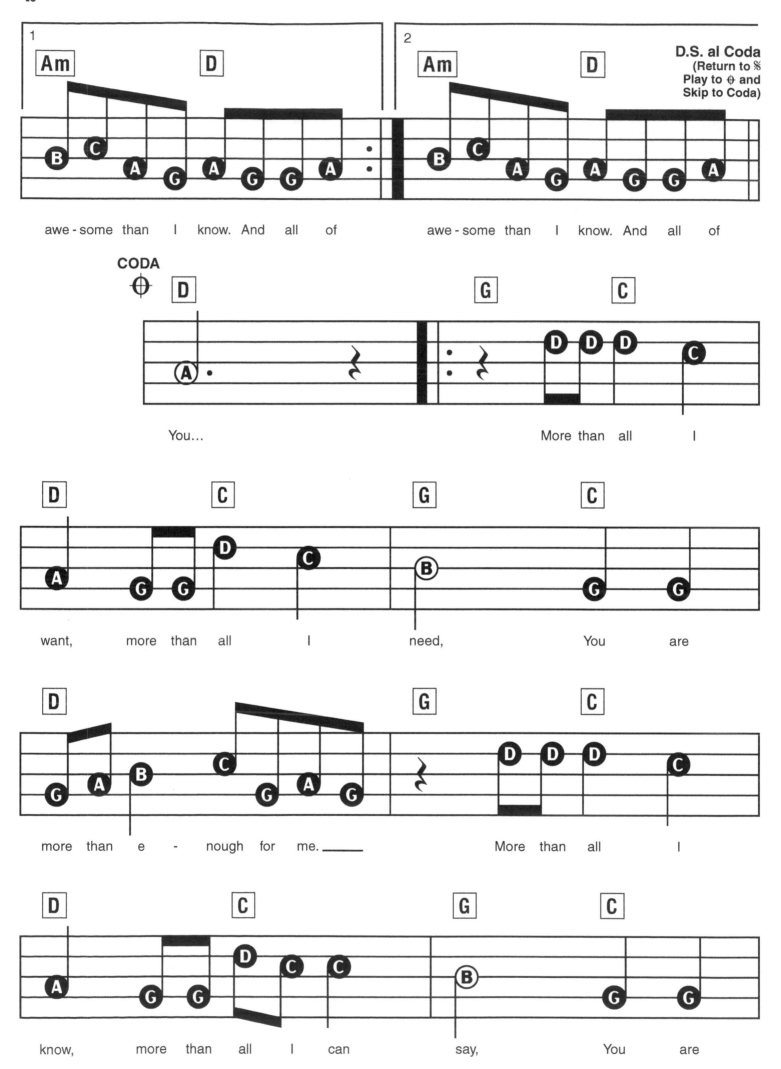

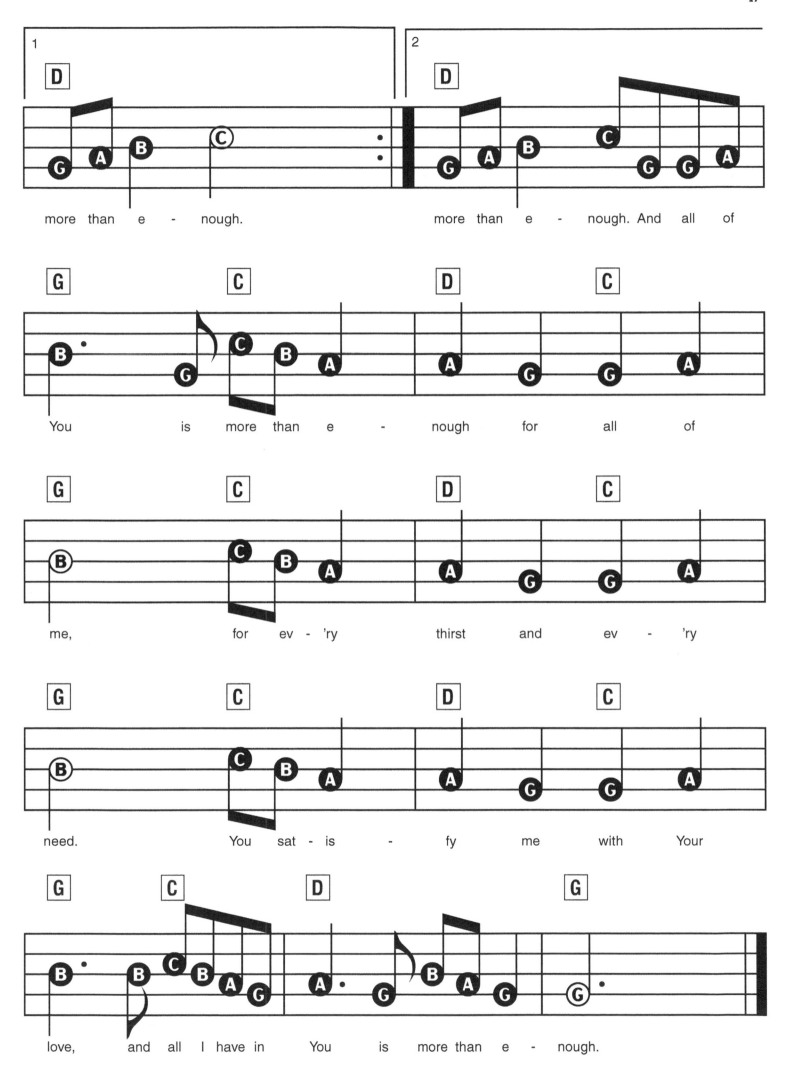

Firm Foundation

Registration 7
Rhythm: 8 Beat or Rock

Words and Music by Nancy Gordon
and Jamie Harvill

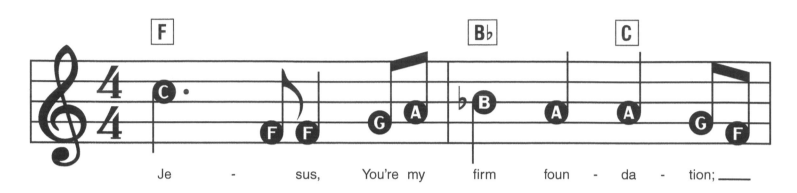

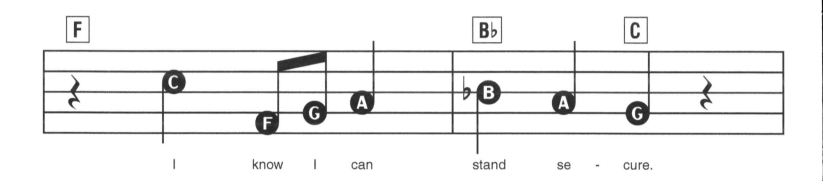

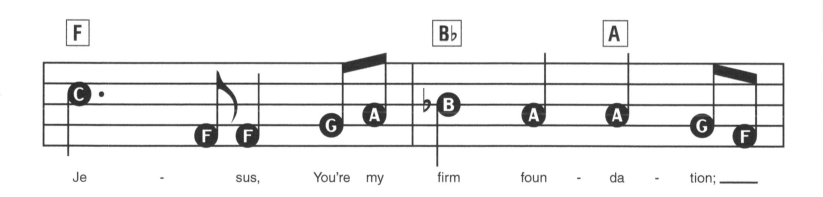

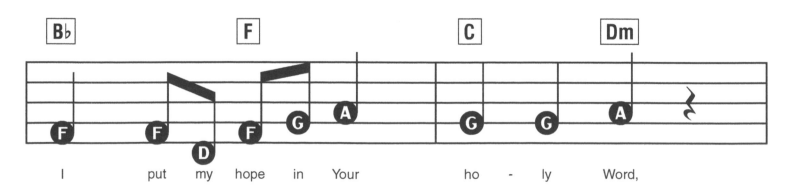

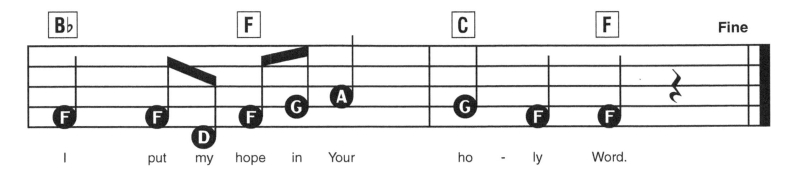

I put my hope in Your ho - ly Word.

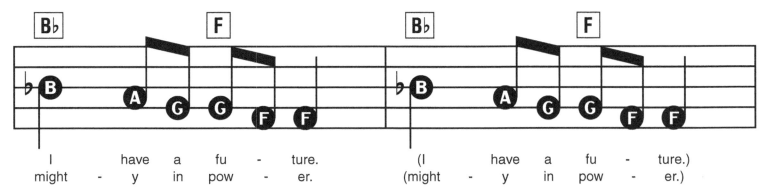

{ I have a liv - ing hope, (I have a liv - ing hope,)
Your Word is faith - ful, (Your Word is faith - ful,)

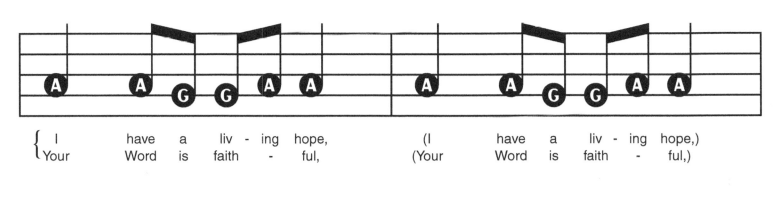

I have a fu - ture. (I have a fu - ture.)
might - y in pow - er. (might - y in pow - er.)

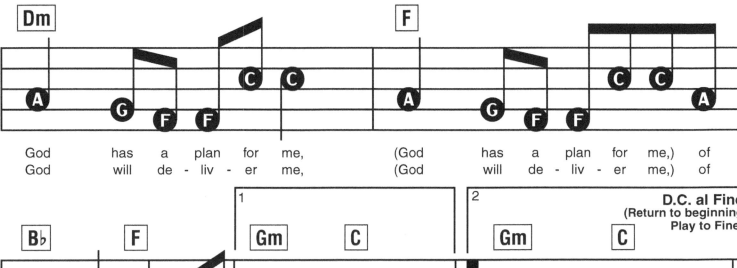

God has a plan for me, (God has a plan for me,) of
God will de - liv - er me, (God will de - liv - er me,) of

D.C. al Fine
(Return to beginning
Play to Fine)

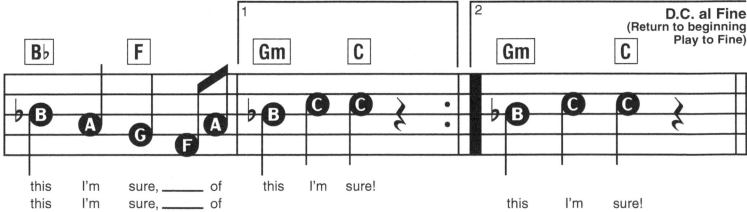

this I'm sure, _____ of this I'm sure!
this I'm sure, _____ of   this I'm sure!

Forever

Registration 2
Rhythm: 8 Beat or Rock

Words and Music by
Chris Tomlin

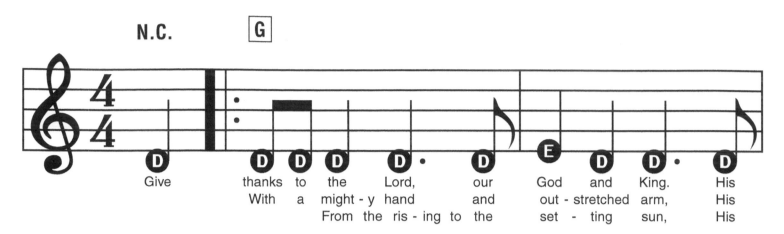

Give thanks to the Lord, our God and King. His
With a might - y hand and out - stretched arm, His
From the ris - ing to the set - ting sun, His

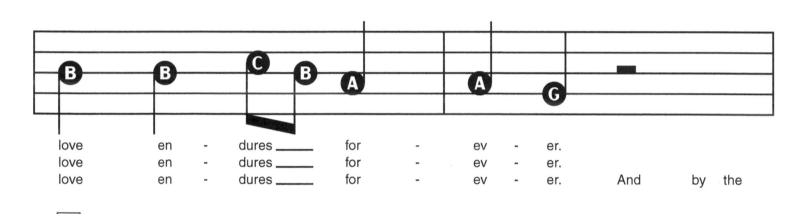

love en - dures _____ for - ev - er.
love en - dures _____ for - ev - er.
love en - dures _____ for - ev - er. And by the

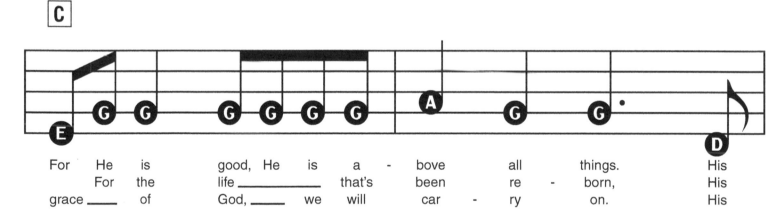

For He is good, He is a - bove all things. His
For the life _____ that's been re - born, His
grace _____ of God, _____ we will car - ry on. His

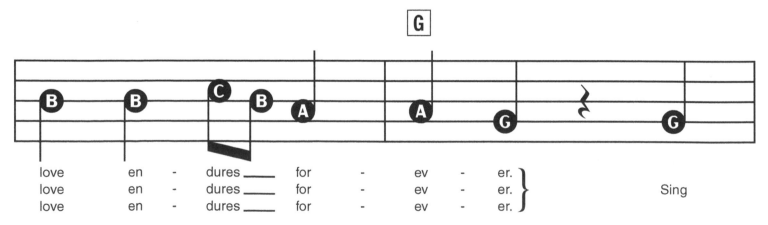

love en - dures _____ for - ev - er.
love en - dures _____ for - ev - er.
love en - dures _____ for - ev - er.

Sing

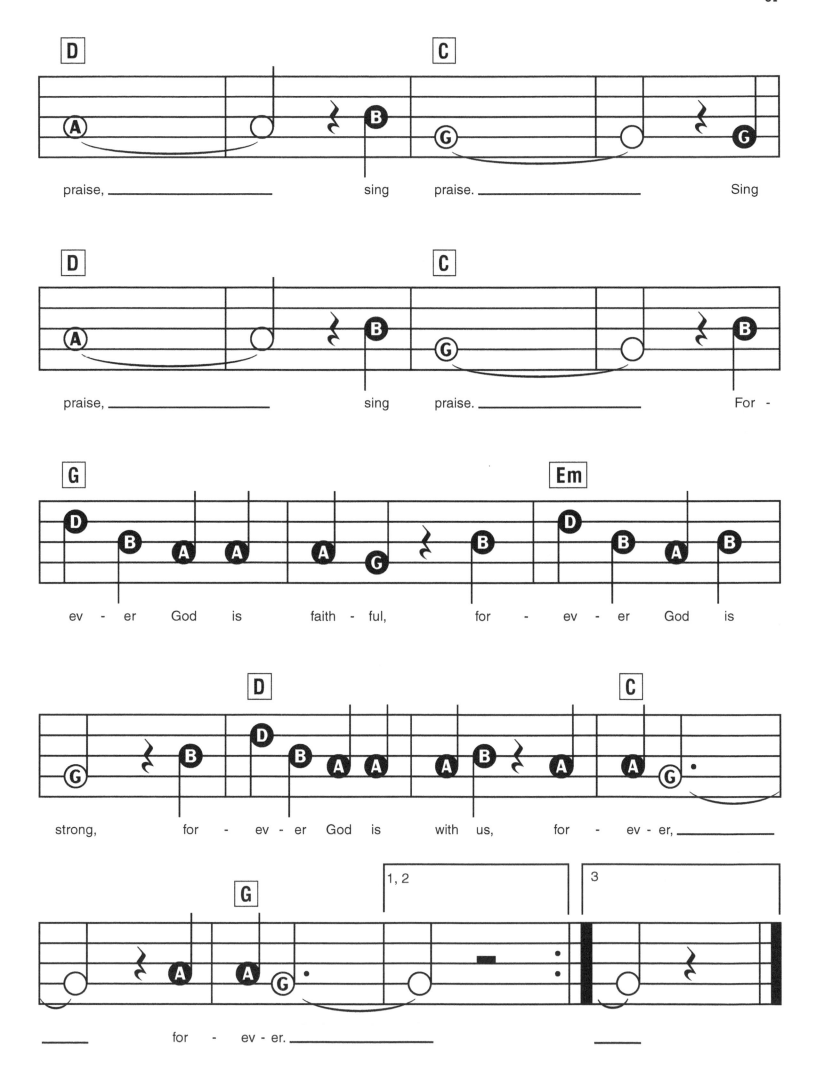

Glorify Thy Name

Registration 3
Rhythm: Ballad

Words and Music by
Donna Adkins

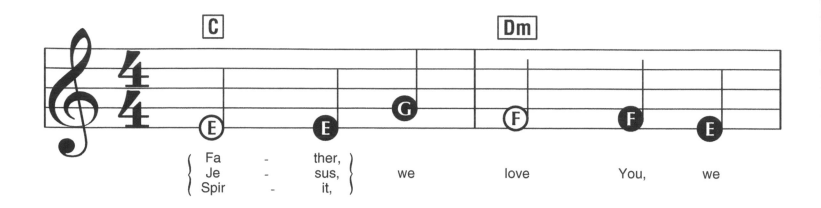

Fa - ther,
Je - sus,
Spir - it,
we love You, we

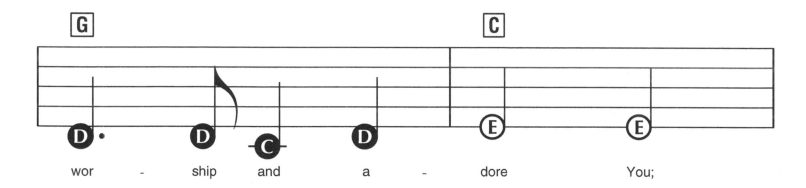

wor - ship and a - dore You;

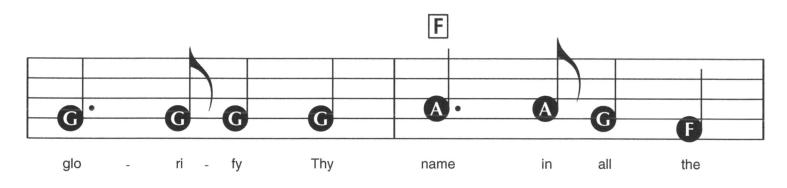

glo - ri - fy Thy name in all the

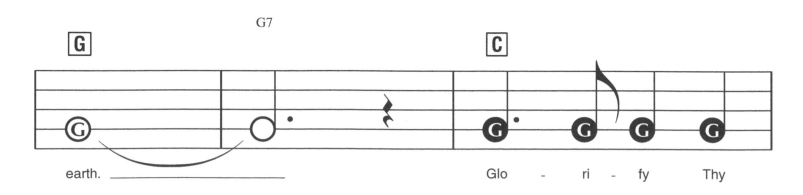

earth. _____ Glo - ri - fy Thy

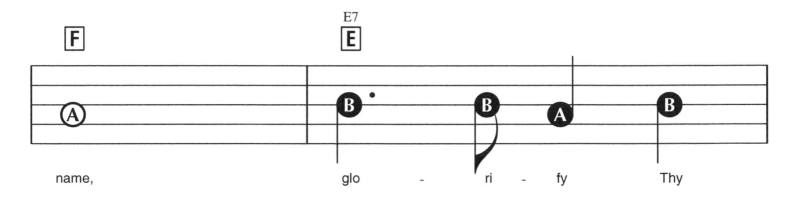

name,

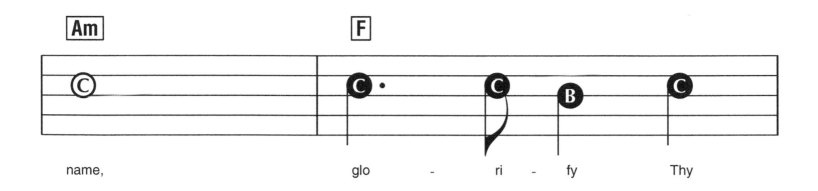

glo - ri - fy Thy

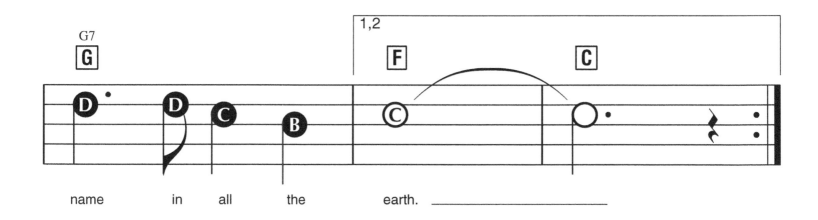

name, glo - ri - fy Thy

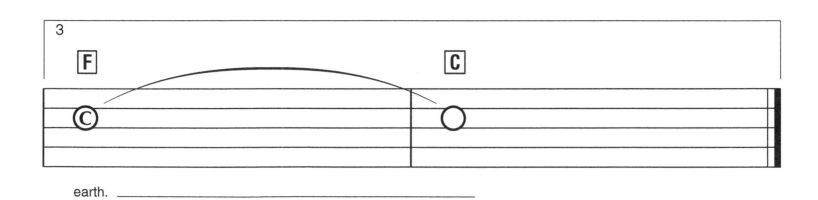

name in all the earth. _____

earth. _____

Great Is the Lord

Registration 5
Rhythm: Waltz

Words and Music by Michael W. Smith
and Deborah D. Smith

C   **Dm**   **G**

E   D   E   F   F E   G   D   F

Great is the Lord, He is ho - ly and

C   **F**   **G**   **F**

E   E D   C   F   E   D   C B   C

just, by His pow - er we trust in His love. _____

C   **Dm**   **G**

E   D   E   F   F E   G   D   F

Great is the Lord, He is faith - ful and

C   **F**   **G**   **F**

E   E D   C   F   E   D   C B   C

true, by His mer - cy He proves He is love. _____

C   **%** **Gm**   **F**

Bb   Bb   A   Bb   Bb   A   G   F

Great is the Lord, and wor - thy of
D.S. Great are You Lord, and wor - thy of

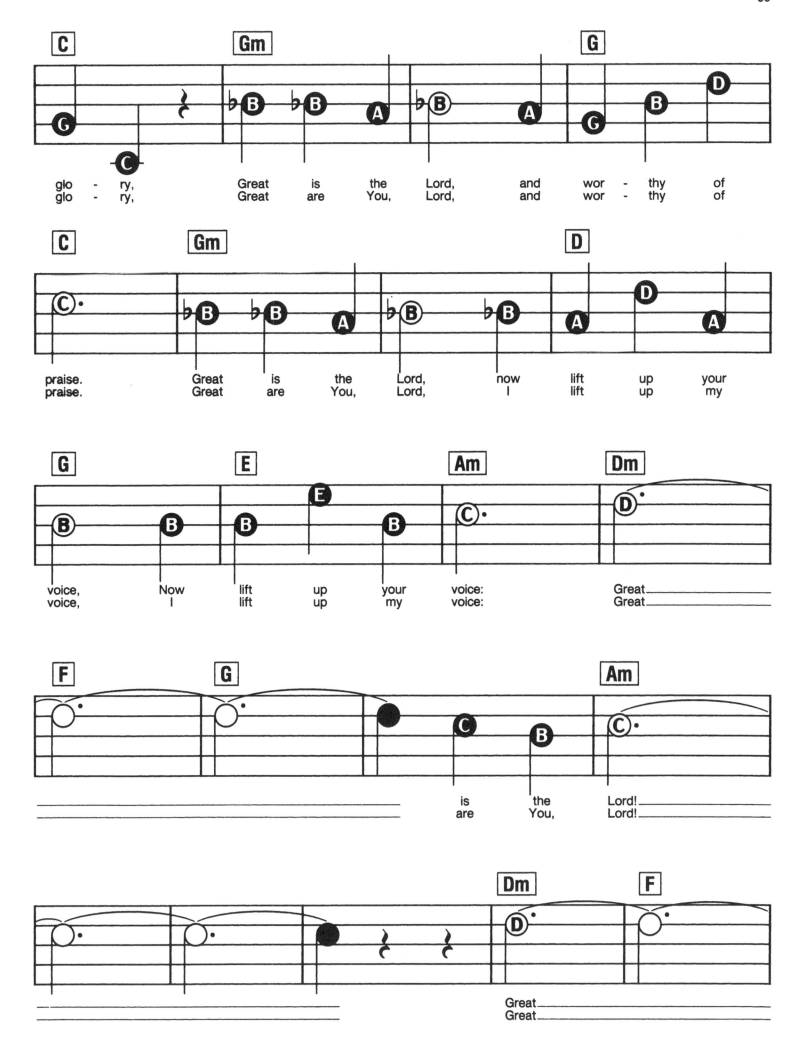

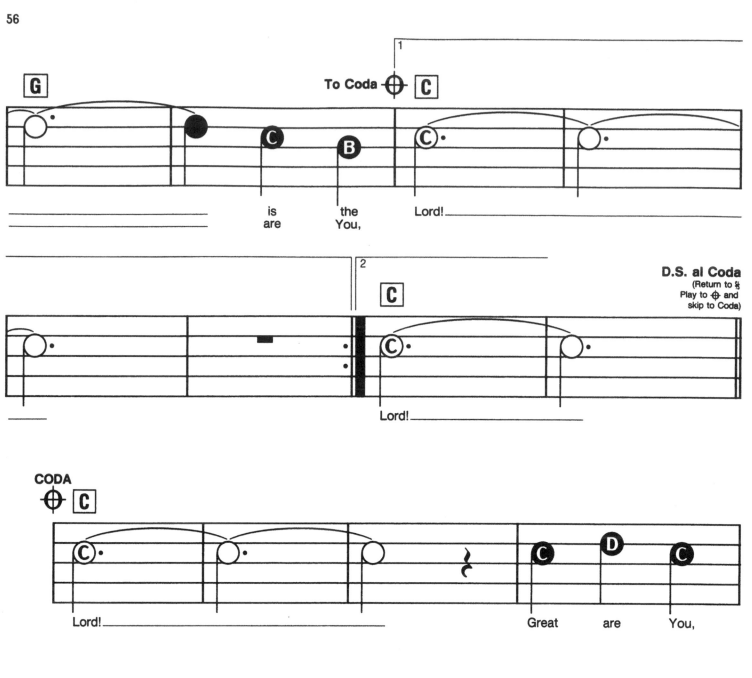

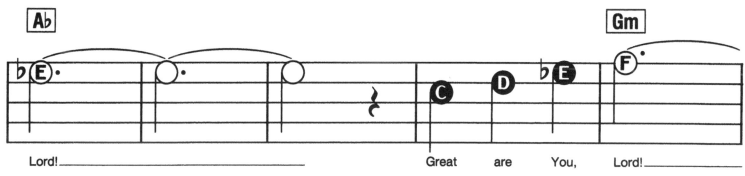

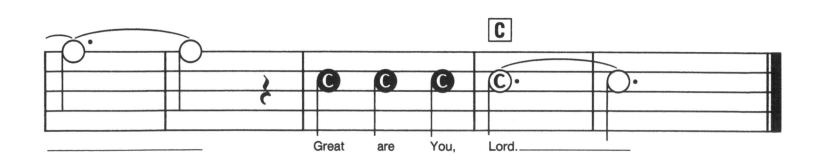

He Is Exalted

Registration 10
Rhythm: Waltz

Words and Music by
Twila Paris

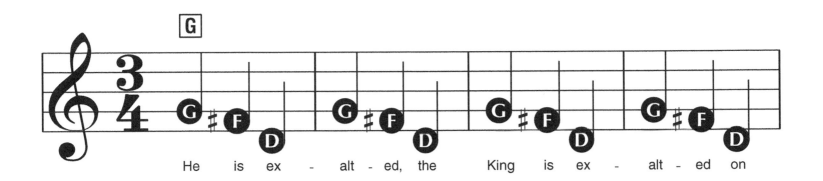

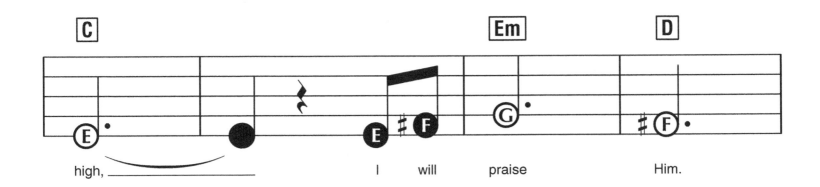

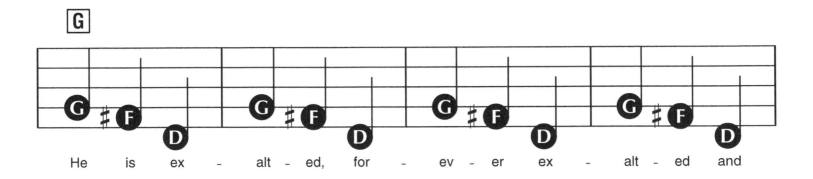

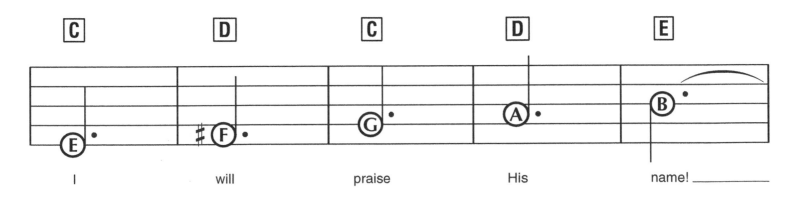

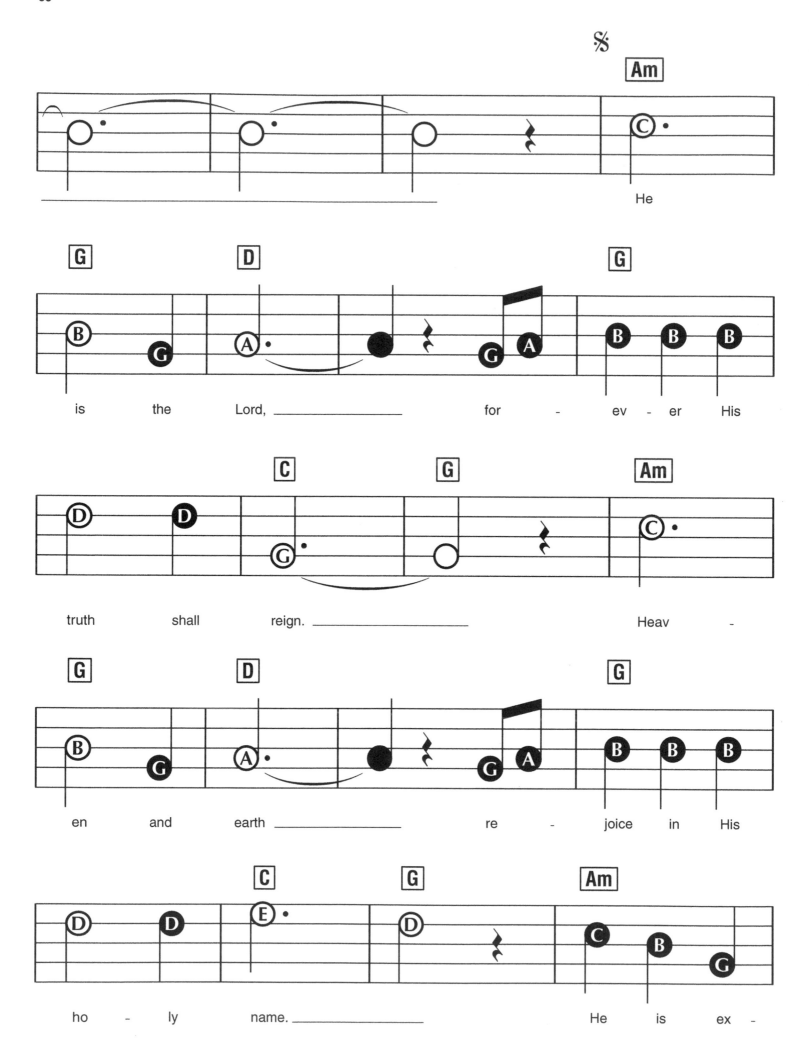

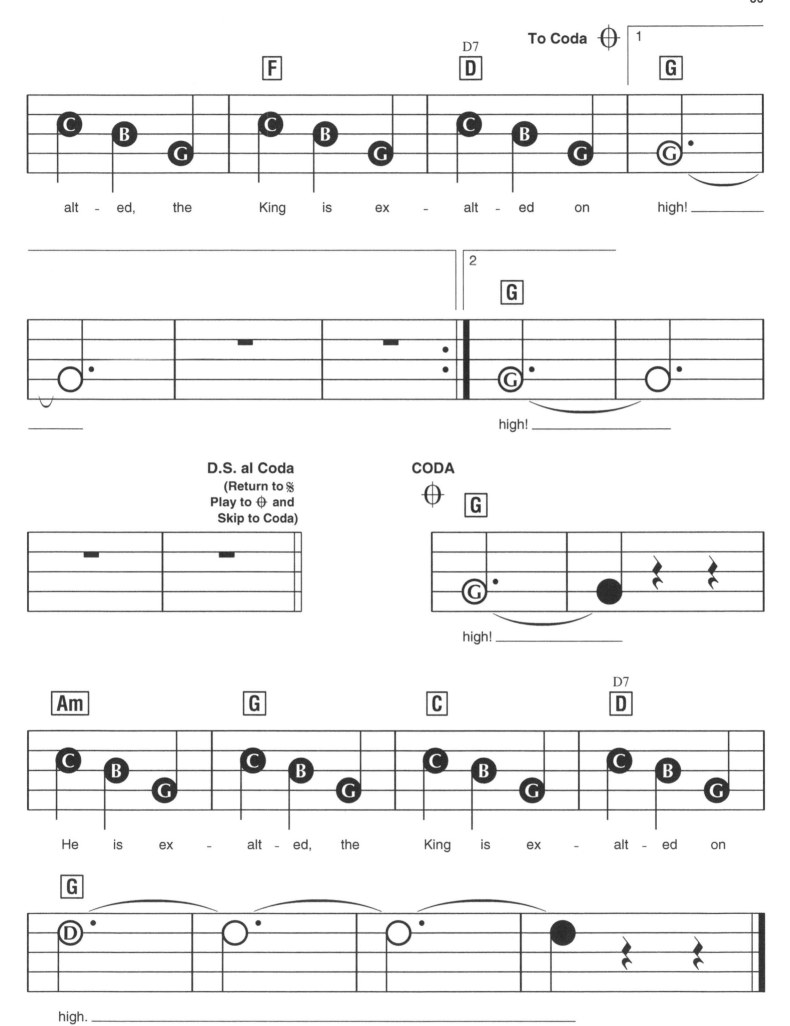

He Has Made Me Glad

Registration 7
Rhythm: Fox Trot

Words and Music by
Leona Von Brethorst

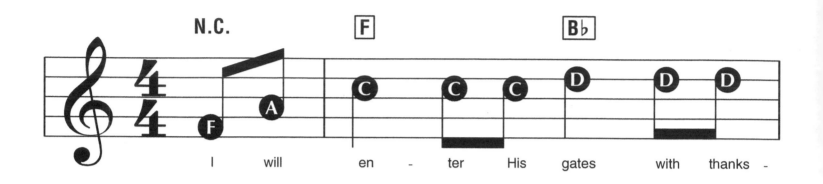

I will en - ter His gates with thanks -

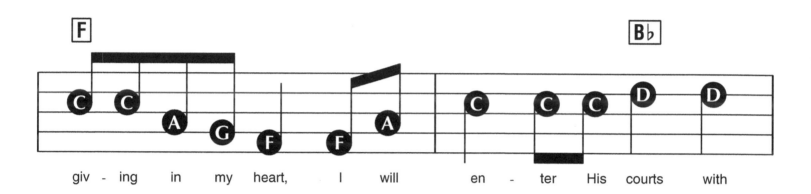

giv - ing in my heart, I will en - ter His courts with

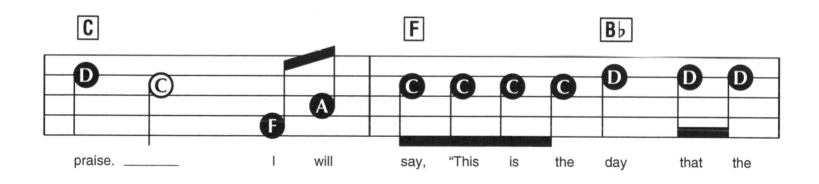

praise. _____ I will say, "This is the day that the

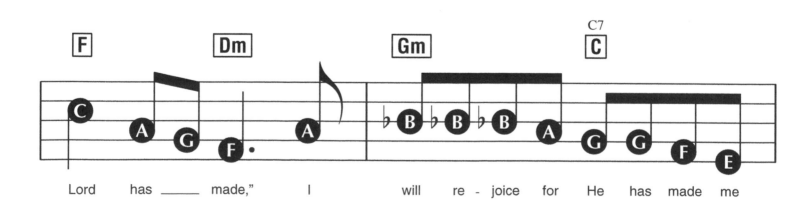

Lord has _____ made," I will re - joice for He has made me

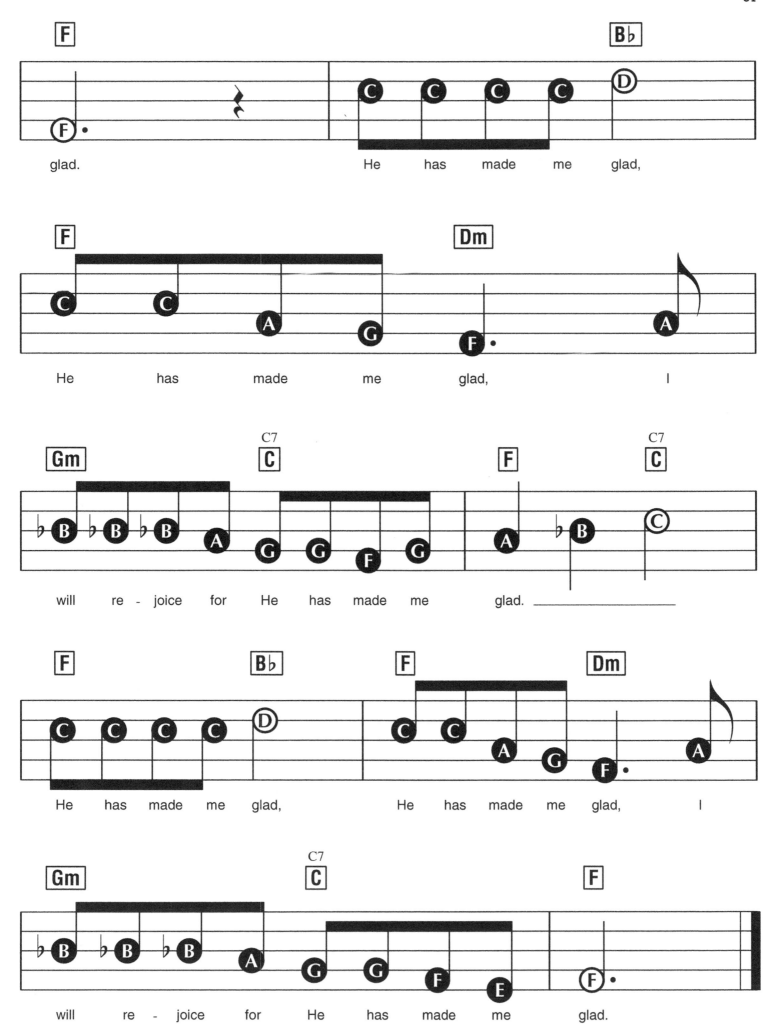

The Heart of Worship

Registration 1
Rhythm: Ballad or 8 Beat

Words and Music by
Matt Redman

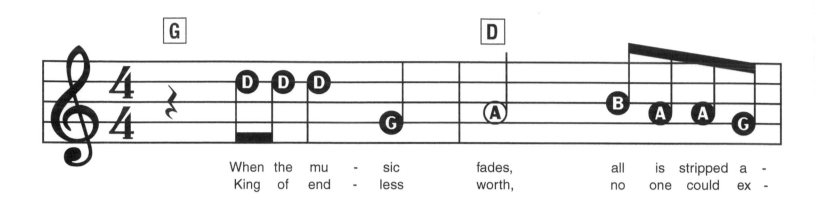

When the mu - sic fades, all is stripped a -
King of end - less worth, no one could ex -

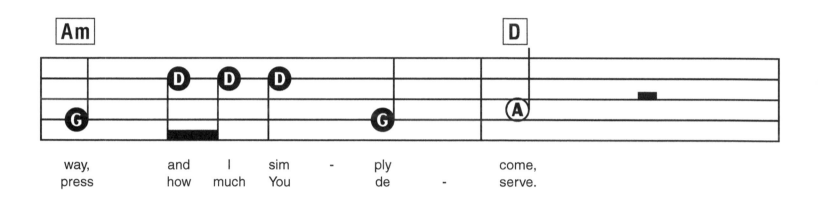

way, and I sim - ply come,
press how much You de - serve.

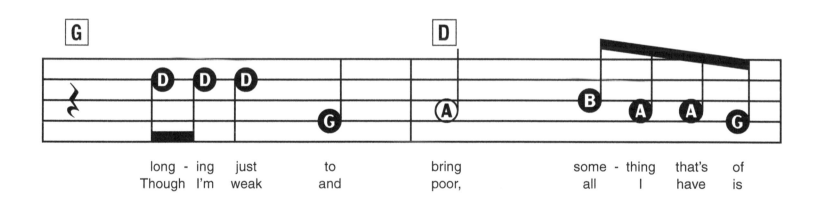

long - ing just to bring some - thing that's of
Though I'm weak and poor, all I have is

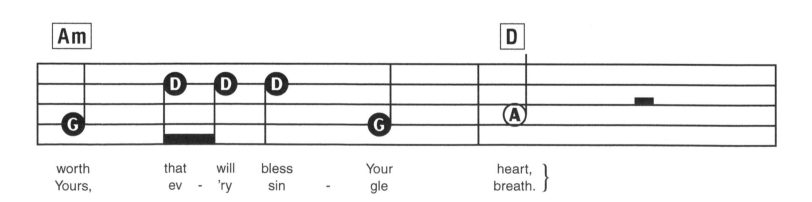

worth that will bless Your heart,
Yours, ev - 'ry sin - gle breath.

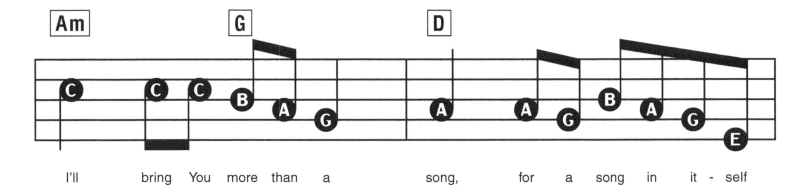

I'll bring You more than a song, for a song in it - self

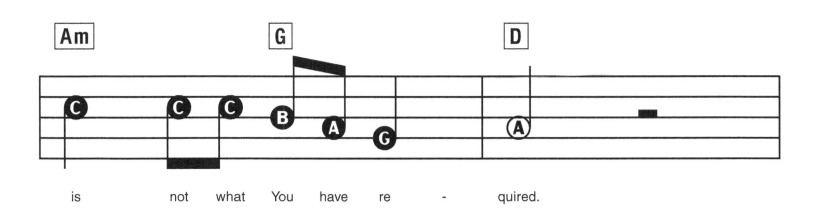

is not what You have re - quired.

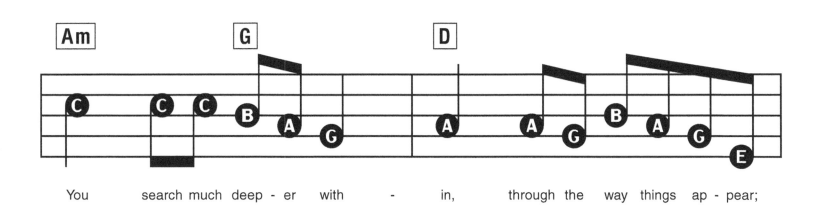

You search much deep - er with - in, through the way things ap - pear;

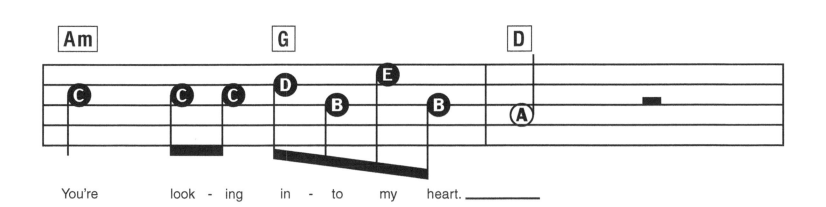

You're look - ing in - to my heart. _____

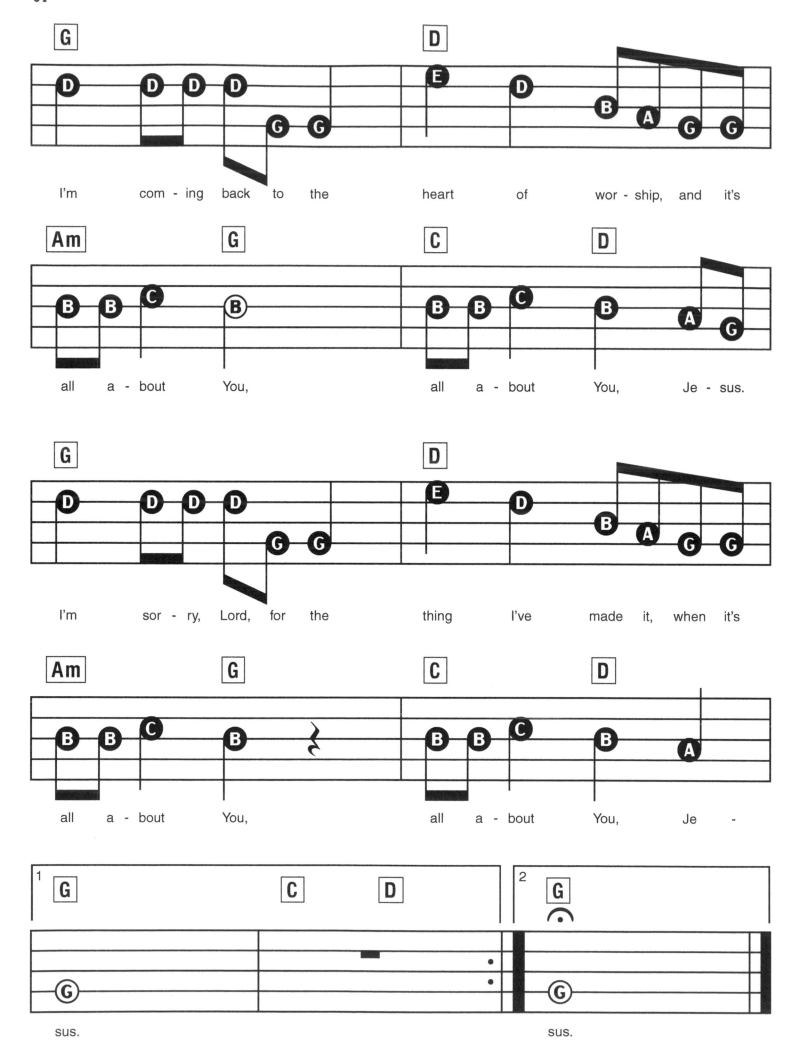

Here I Am to Worship

Registration 4
Rhythm: Ballad or 8 Beat

Words and Music by
Tim Hughes

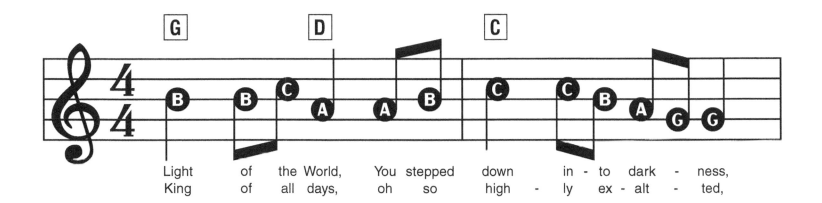

Light of the World, You stepped down in - to dark - ness,
King of all days, oh so high - ly ex - alt - ed,

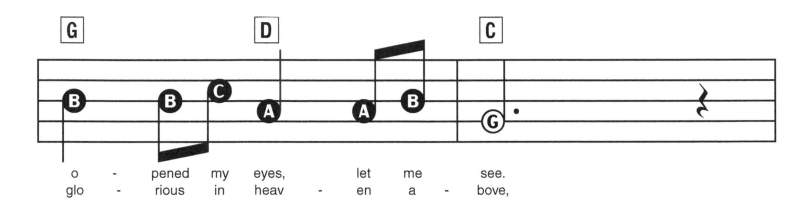

o - pened my eyes, let me see.
glo - rious in heav - en a - bove,

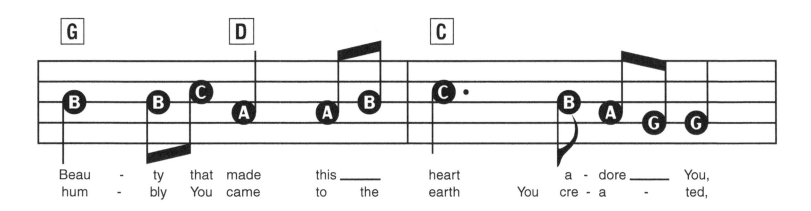

Beau - ty that made this _____ heart a - dore _____ You,
hum - bly You came to the earth You cre - a - ted,

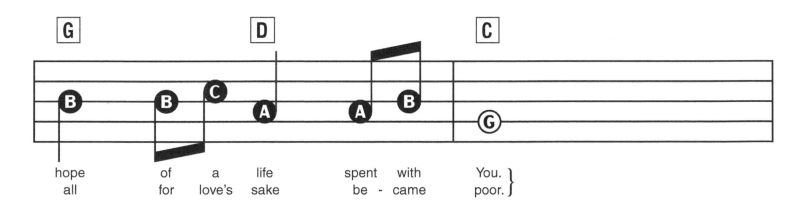

hope of a life spent with You.
all for love's sake be - came poor.

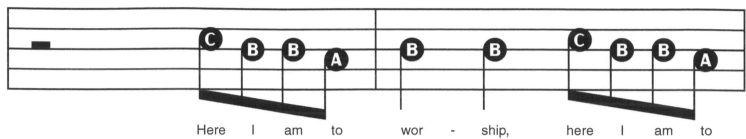

Here I am to wor - ship, here I am to

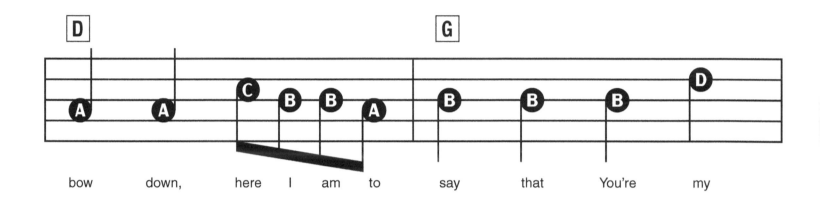

bow down, here I am to say that You're my

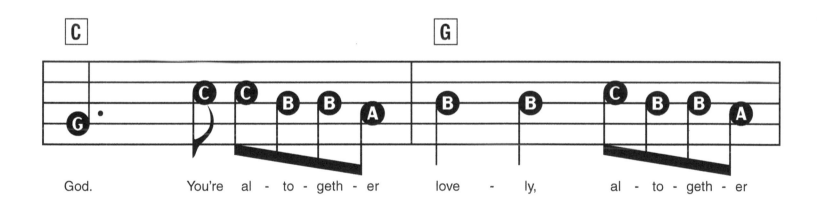

God. You're al - to - geth - er love - ly, al - to - geth - er

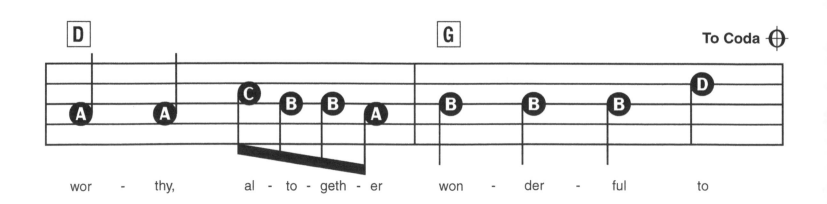

wor - thy, al - to - geth - er won - der - ful to

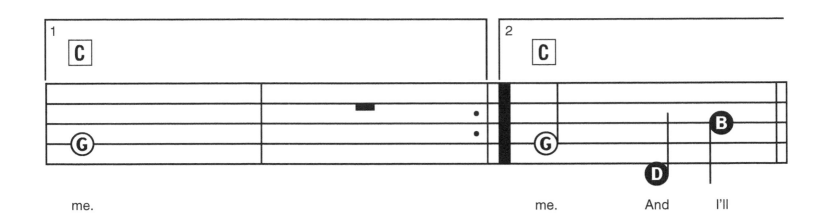

1
C

G

me.

2
C

G

D

B

me.   And   I'll

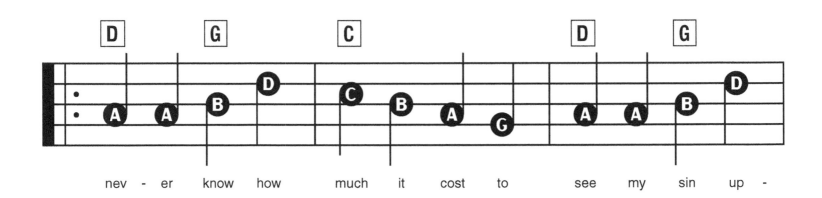

D   G   C   D   G

A   A   B   D   C   B   A   G   A   A   B   D

nev - er   know   how   much   it   cost   to   see   my   sin   up -

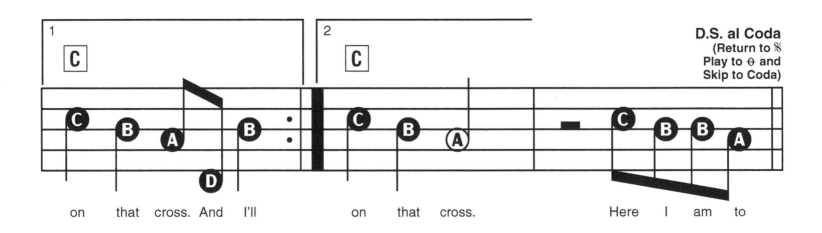

1
C

C   B   A   B   D

on   that   cross.   And   I'll

2
C

D.S. al Coda
(Return to %
Play to ⊕ and
Skip to Coda)

C   B   A

on   that   cross.

C   B   B   A

Here   I   am   to

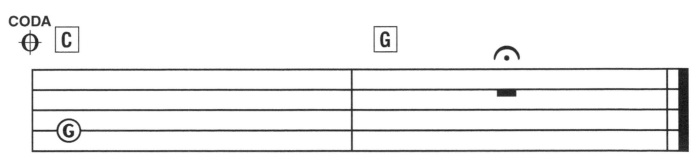

CODA
⊕ C   G

G

me.

Holy and Anointed One

Registration 1
Rhythm: Ballad

Words and Music by
John Barnett

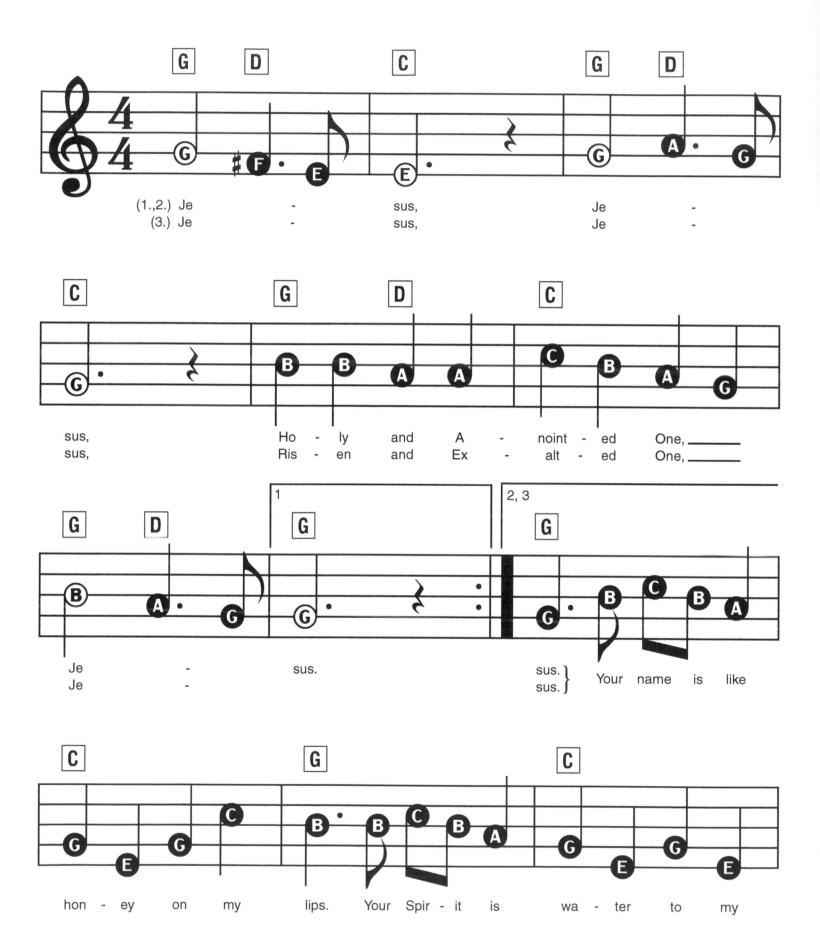

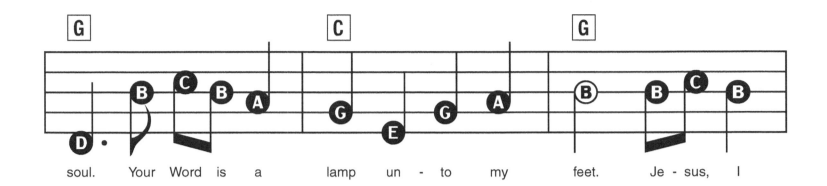

soul. Your Word is a lamp un - to my feet. Je - sus, I

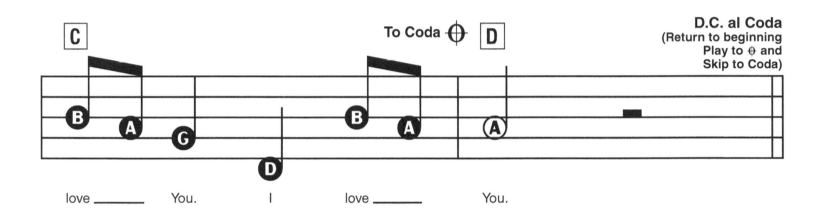

To Coda ⊕

D.C. al Coda
(Return to beginning
Play to ⊕ and
Skip to Coda)

love _____ You. I love _____ You.

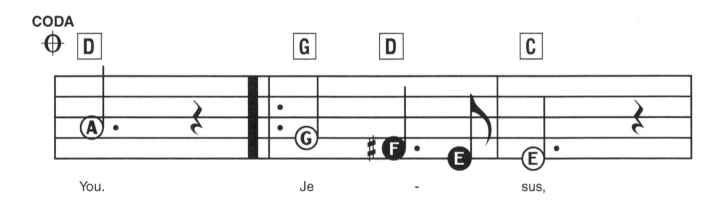

CODA ⊕

You. Je - sus,

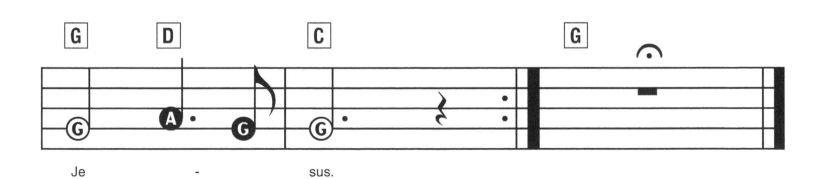

Je - sus.

How Majestic Is Your Name

Registration 5
Rhythm: Rock

Words and Music by
Michael W. Smith

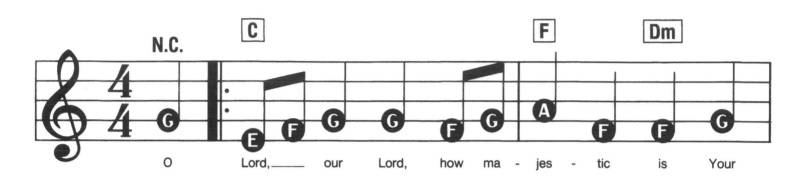

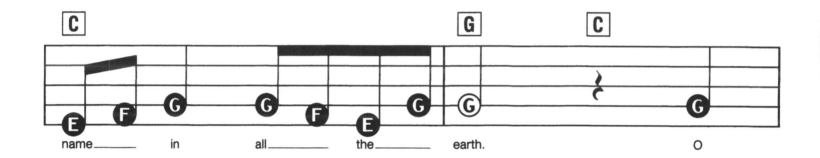

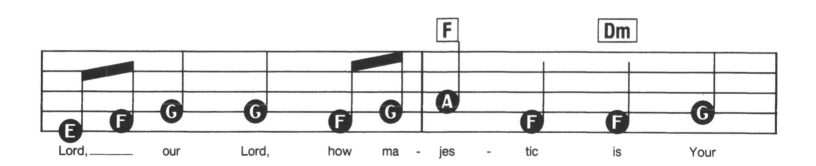

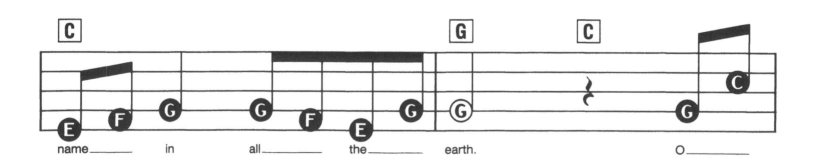

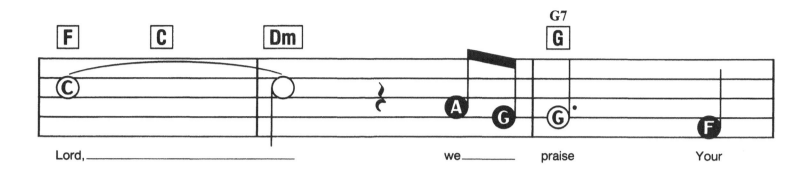

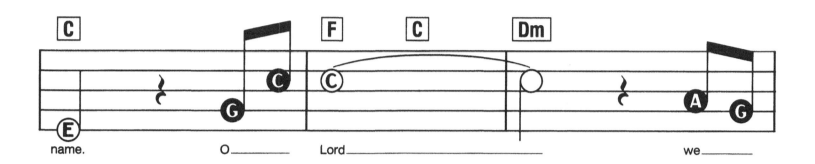

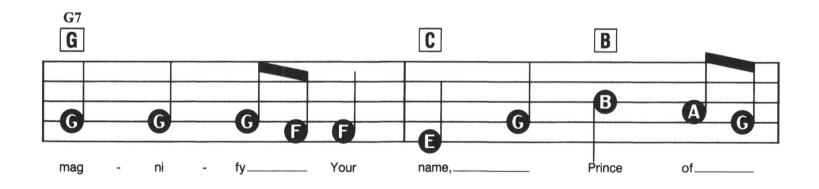

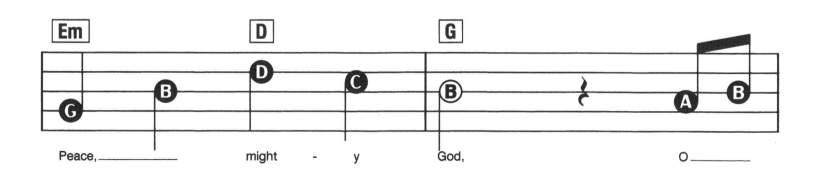

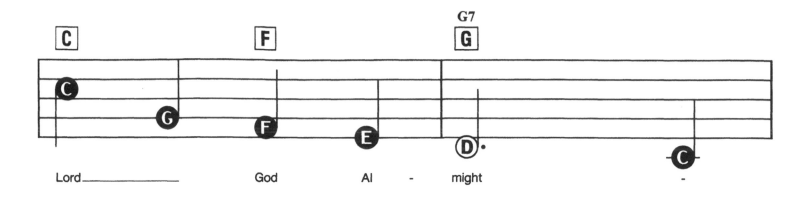

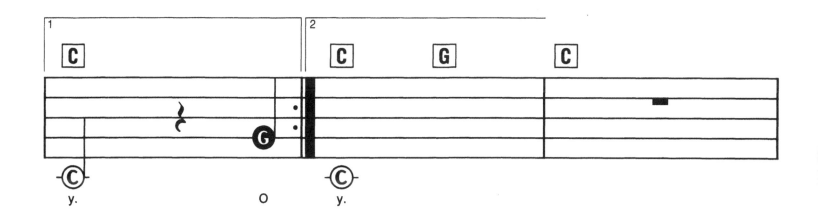

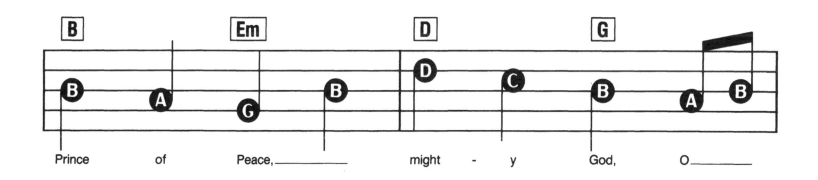

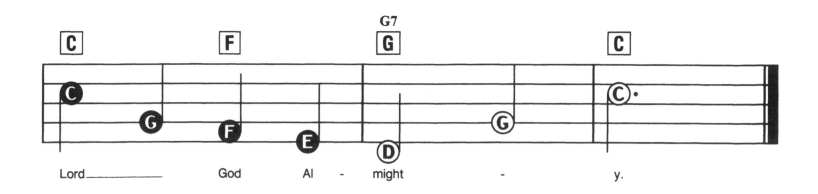

Holy Is the Lord

Registration 4
Rhythm: 8 Beat or Pop

Words and Music by Chris Tomlin
and Louie Giglio

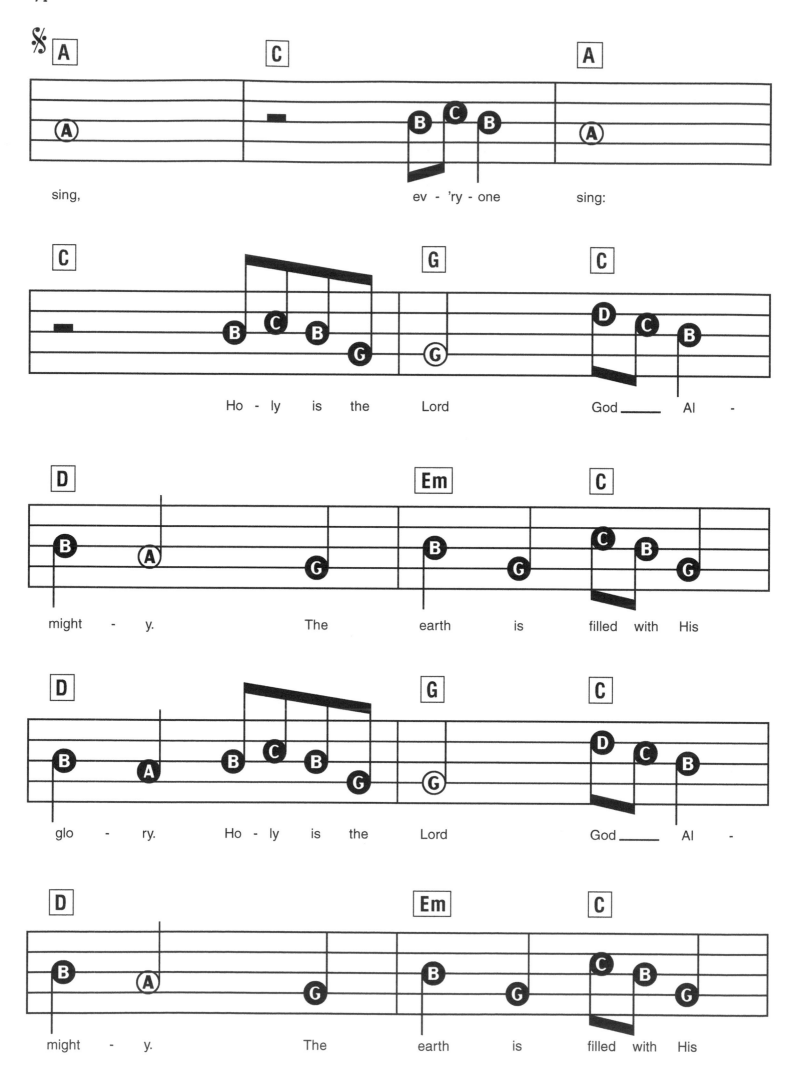

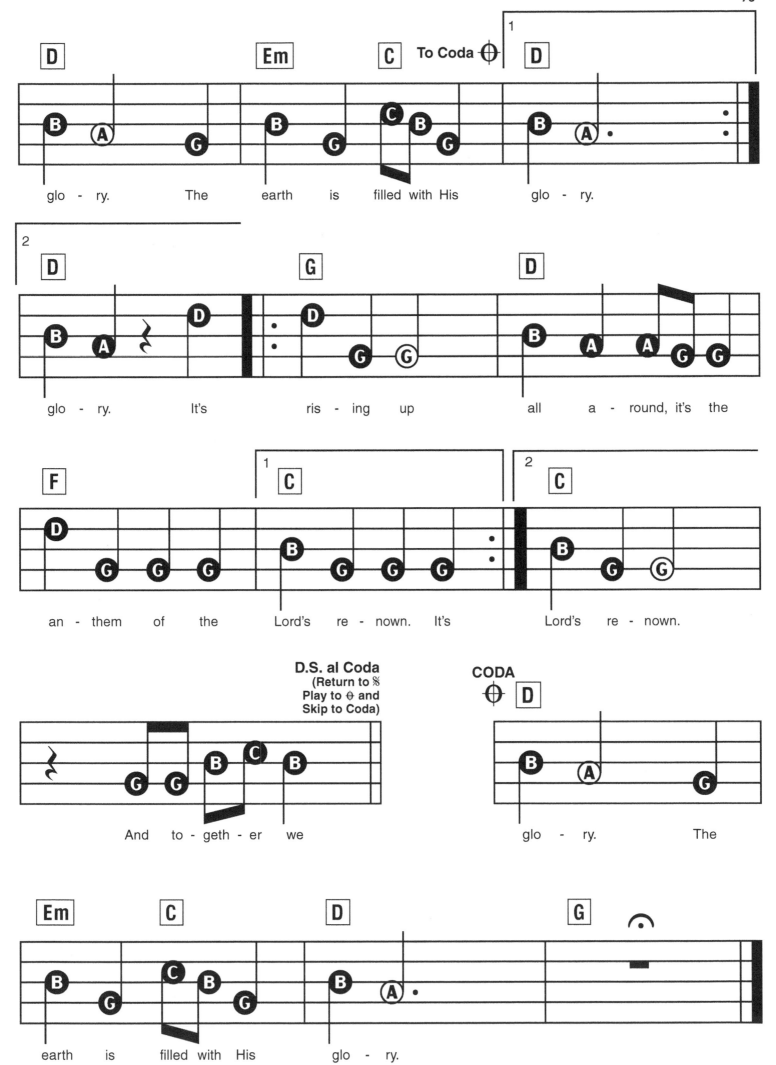

I Could Sing of Your Love Forever

Registration 4
Rhythm: Pop or 8 Beat

Words and Music by
Martin Smith

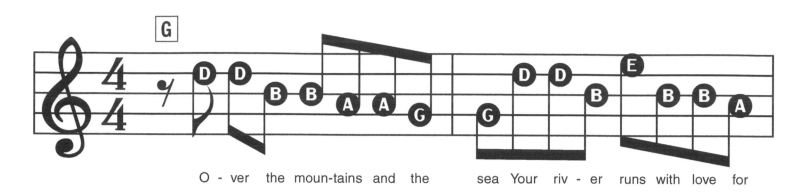

O - ver the moun-tains and the   sea Your riv - er runs with love for

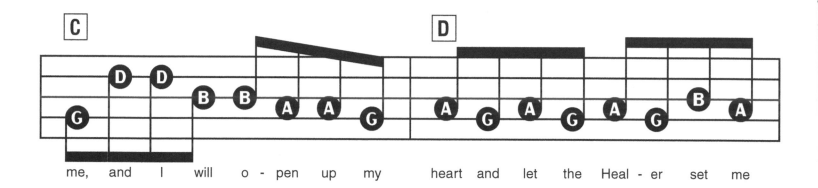

me, and I will o - pen up my   heart and let the Heal - er set me

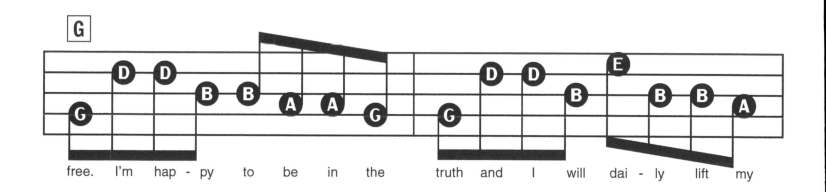

free. I'm hap - py to be in the   truth and I will dai - ly lift my

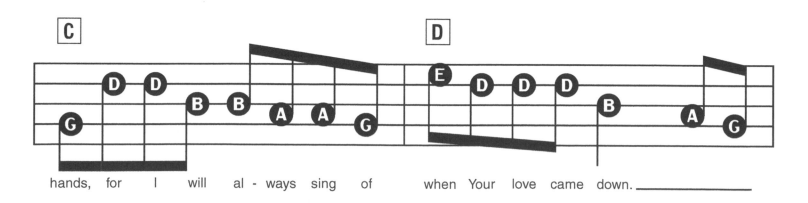

hands, for I will al - ways sing of   when Your love came down. _____

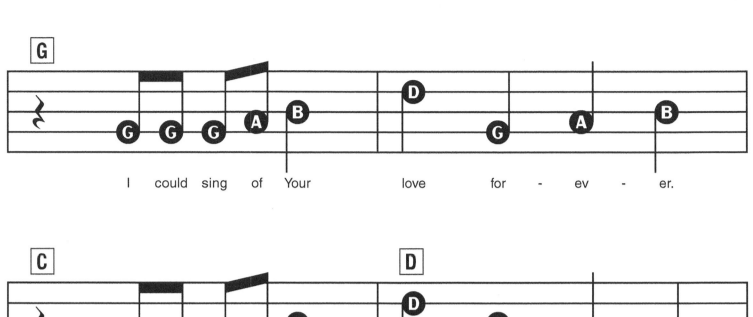

I could sing of Your love for - ev - er.

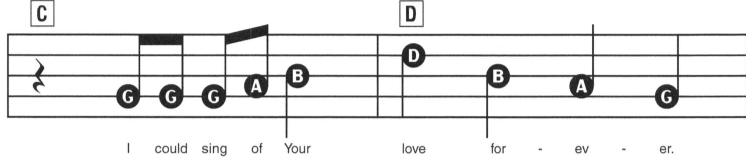

I could sing of Your love for - ev - er.

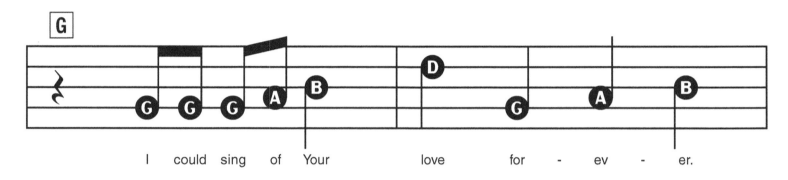

I could sing of Your love for - ev - er.

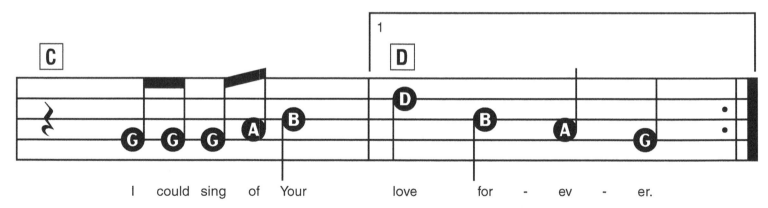

I could sing of Your love for - ev - er.

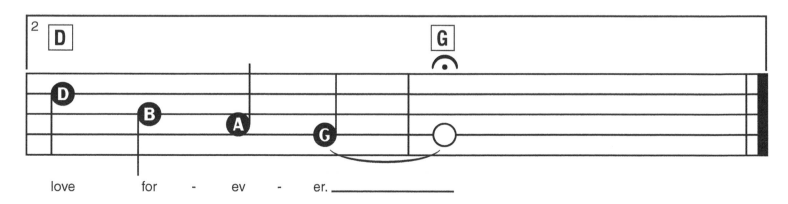

love for - ev - er. _____

I Give You My Heart

Registration 3
Rhythm: Ballad or Pop

Words and Music by
Reuben Morgan

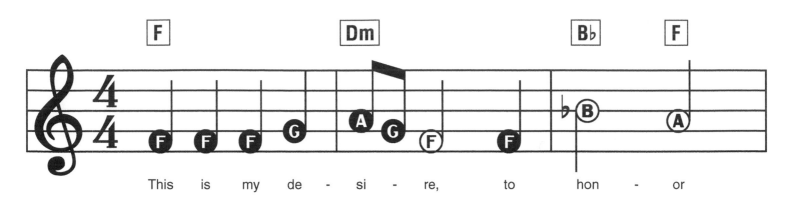

This is my de - si - re, to hon - or

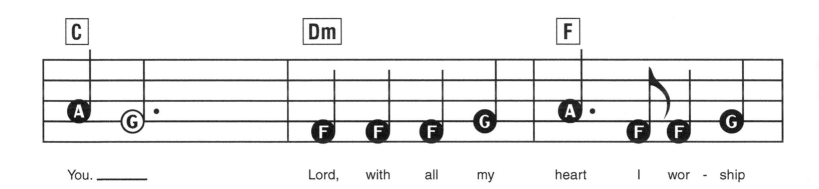

You. _____ Lord, with all my heart I wor - ship

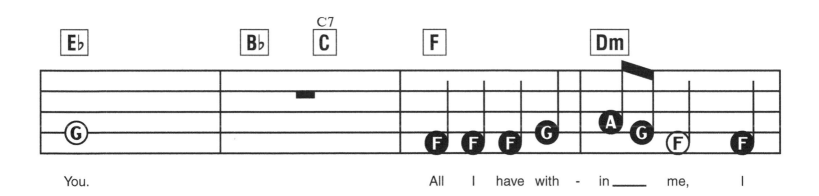

You. All I have with - in ___ me, I

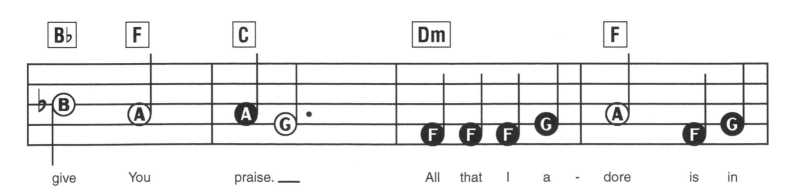

give You praise. ___ All that I a - dore is in

I Love You Lord

Registration 1
Rhythm: Ballad

Words and Music by
Laurie Klein

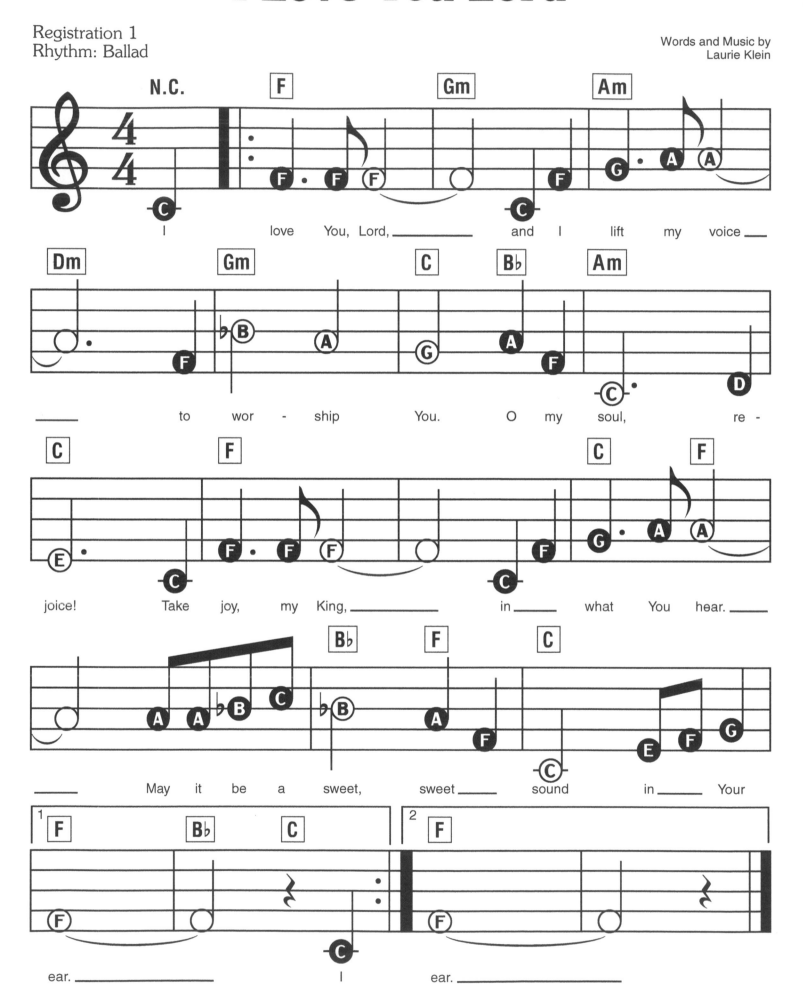

I Stand in Awe

Registration 4
Rhythm: Ballad or 8 Beat

Words and Music by
Mark Altrogge

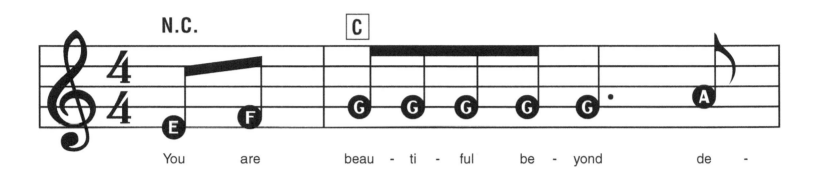

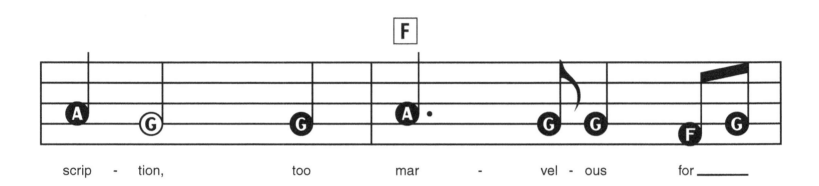

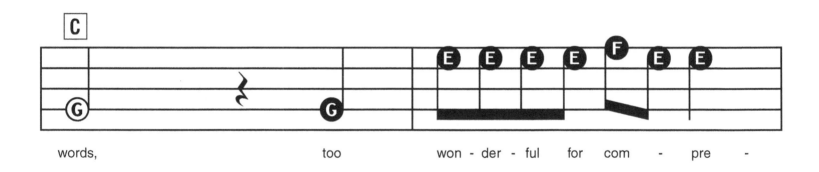

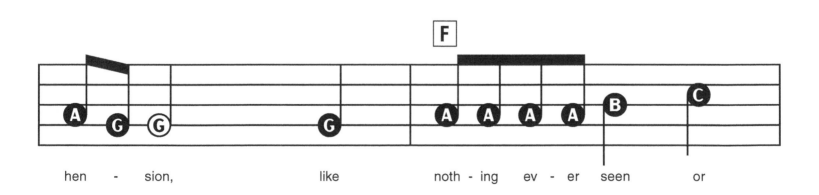

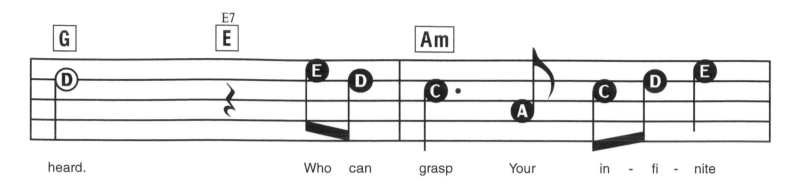

heard. Who can grasp Your in - fi - nite

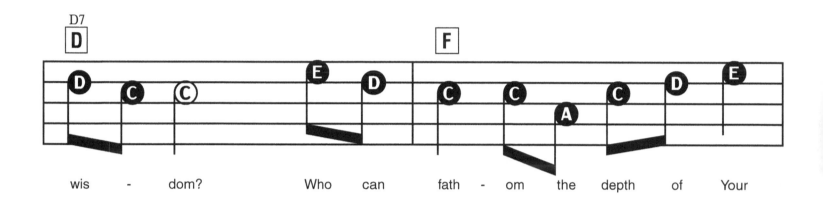

wis - dom? Who can fath - om the depth of Your

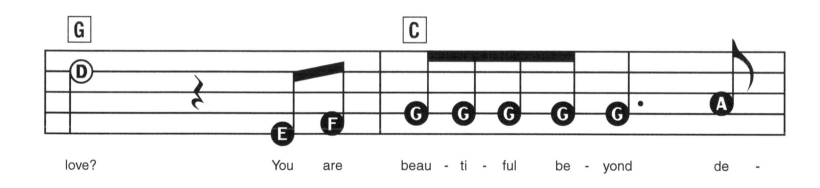

love? You are beau - ti - ful be - yond de -

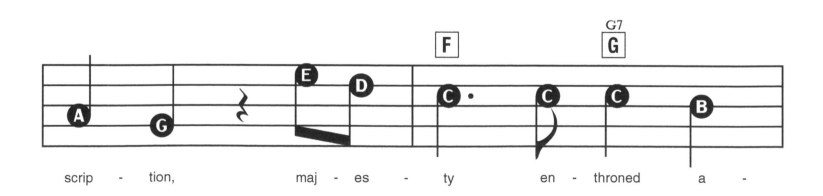

scrip - tion, maj - es - ty en - throned a -

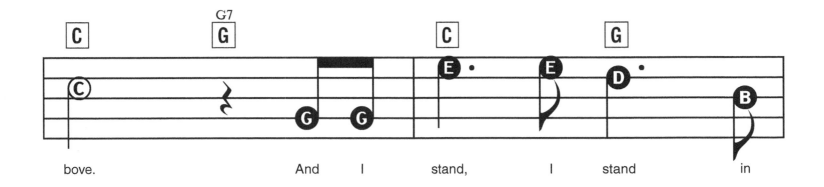

bove.　　　And　I　stand,　I　stand　in

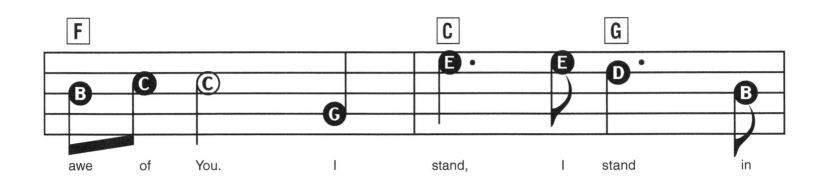

awe　of　You.　　　I　stand,　I　stand　in

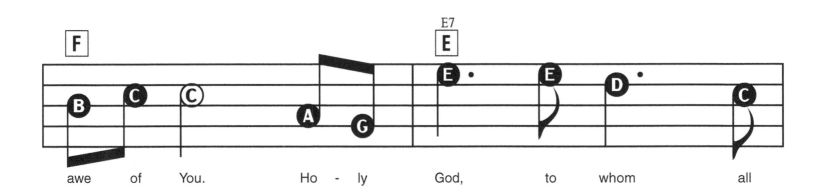

awe　of　You.　　Ho - ly　God,　to　whom　all

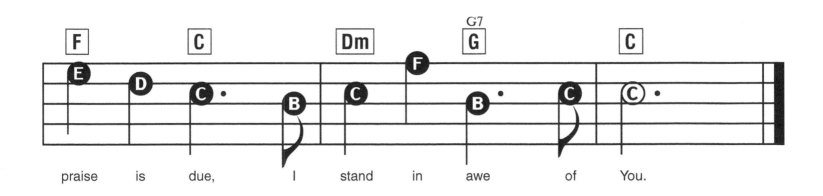

praise　is　due,　I　stand　in　awe　of　You.

I Want to Know You

Registration 1
Rhythm: Ballad or 8 Beat

Words and Music by
Andy Park

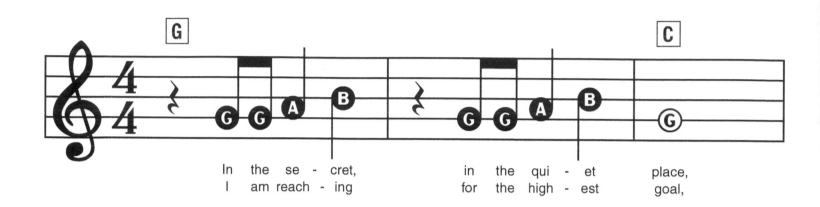

In the se - cret, in the qui - et place,
I am reach - ing for the high - est goal,

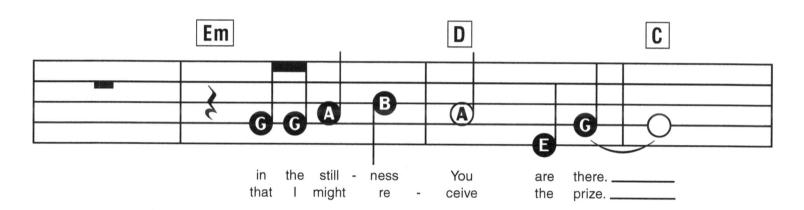

in the still - ness You are there. _____
that I might re - ceive the prize. _____

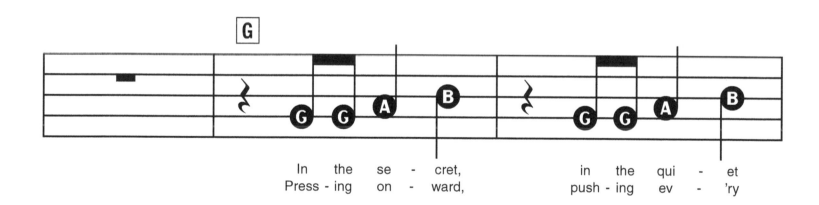

In the se - cret, in the qui - et
Press - ing on - ward, push - ing ev - 'ry

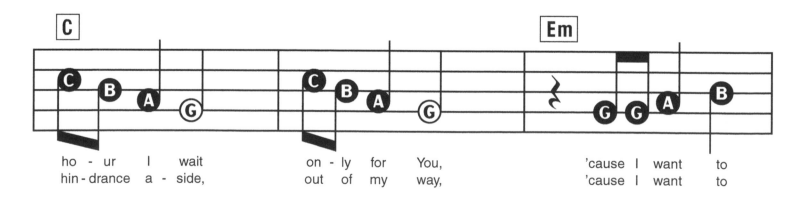

ho - ur I wait on - ly for You, 'cause I want to
hin - drance a - side, out of my way, 'cause I want to

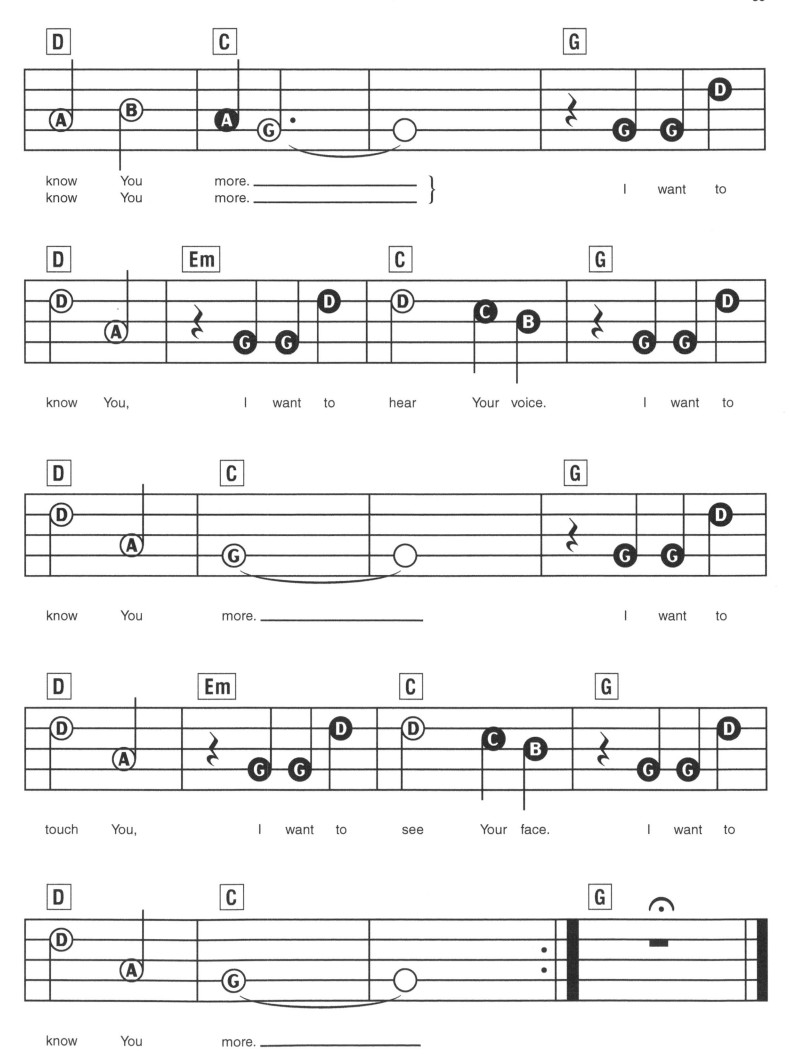

I Worship You, Almighty God

Registration 2
Rhythm: Ballad or 8 Beat

Words and Music by
Sondra Corbett-Wood

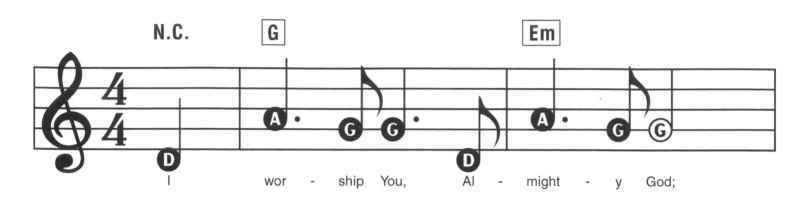

I wor - ship You, Al - might - y God;

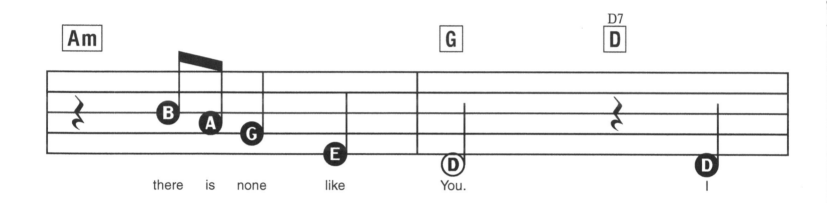

there is none like You. wor -

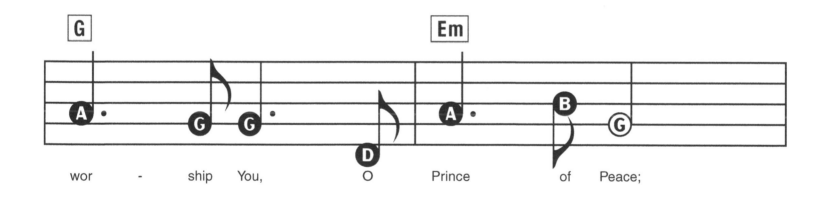

wor - ship You, O Prince of Peace;

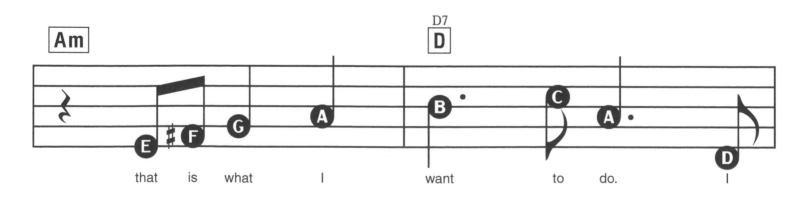

that is what I want to do. I

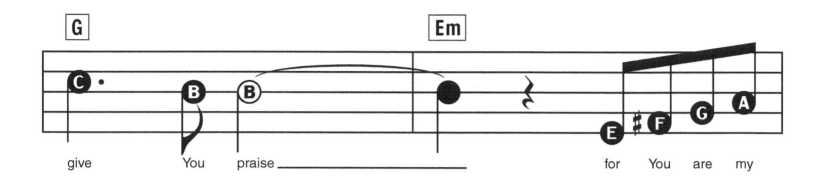

give You praise _____ for You are my

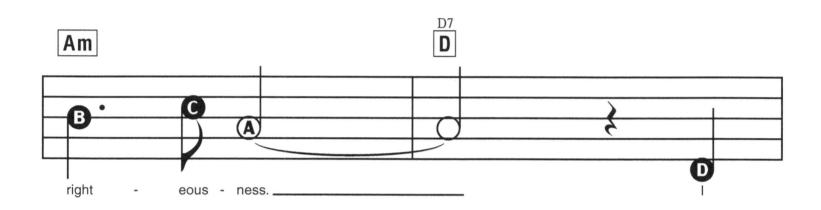

right - eous - ness. _____ I

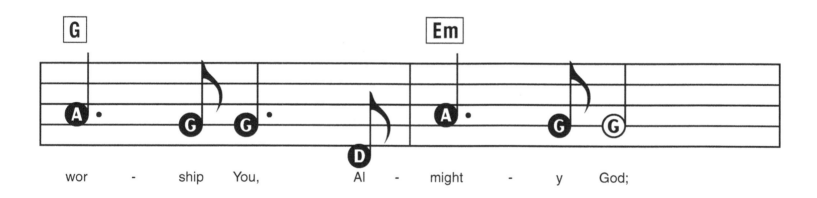

wor - ship You, Al - might - y God;

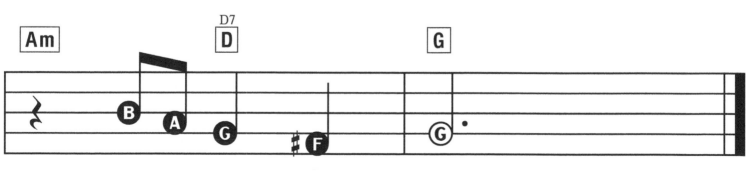

there is none like You.

Jesus, Lover of My Soul

Registration 8
Rhythm: Ballad or Pop

Words and Music by John Ezzy,
Daniel Grul and Stephen McPherson

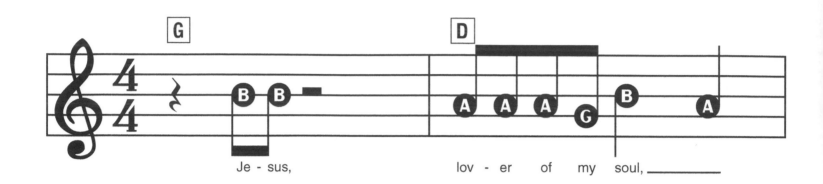

Je - sus, lov - er of my soul, _____

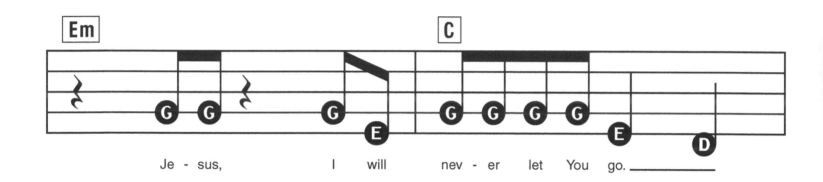

Je - sus, I will nev - er let You go. _____

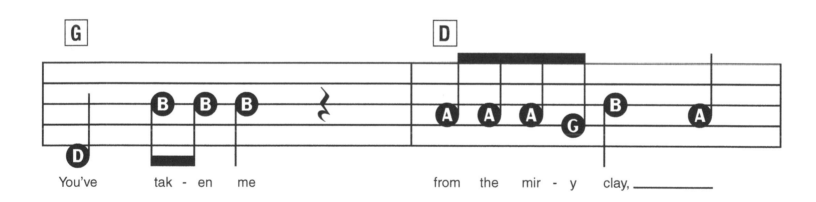

You've tak - en me from the mir - y clay, _____

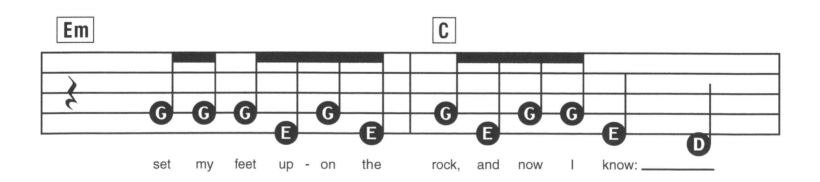

set my feet up - on the rock, and now I know: _____

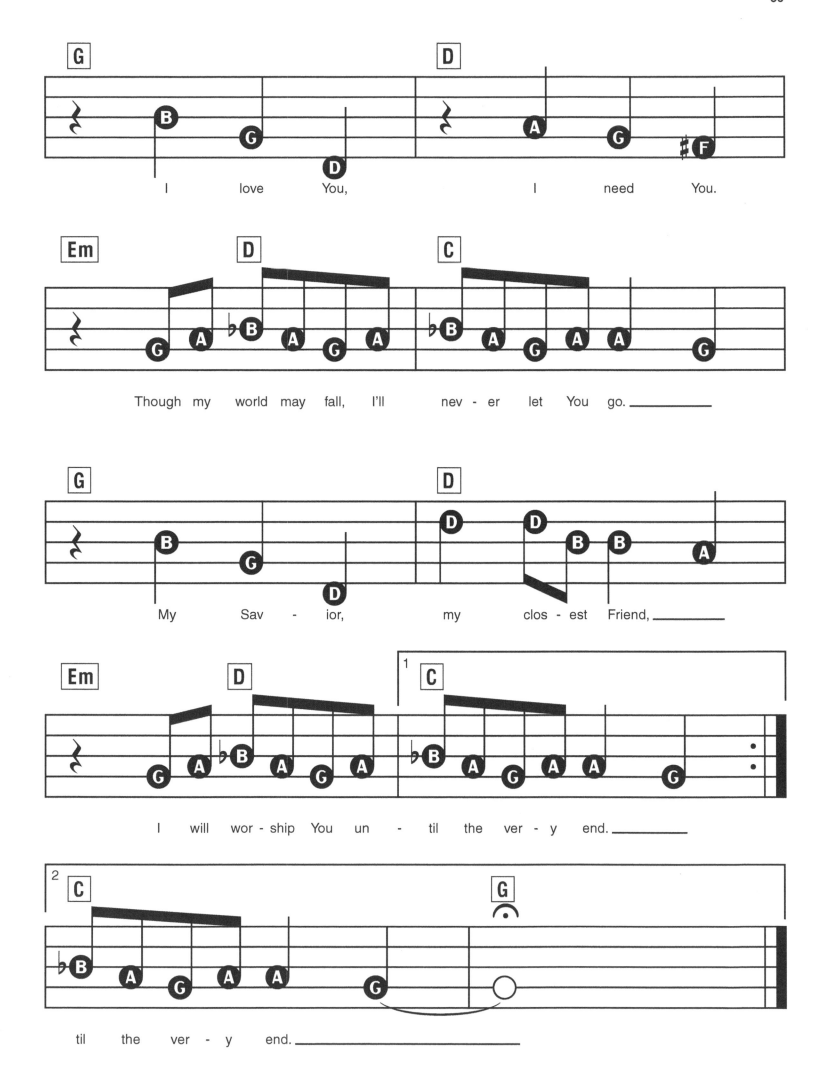

Jesus, Name Above All Names

Registration 1
Rhythm: Waltz

Words and Music by
Naida Hearn

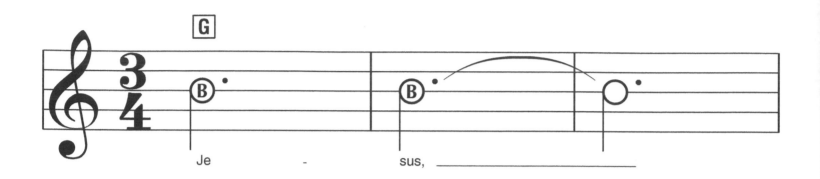

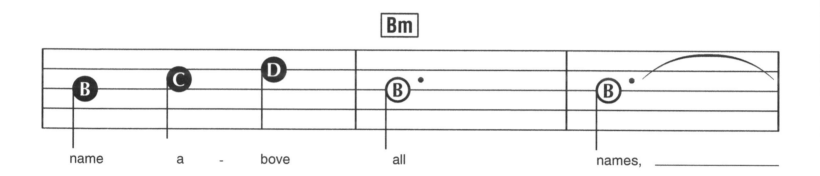

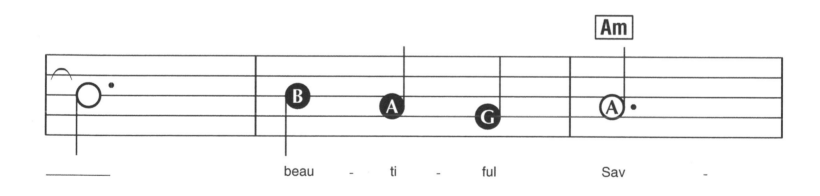

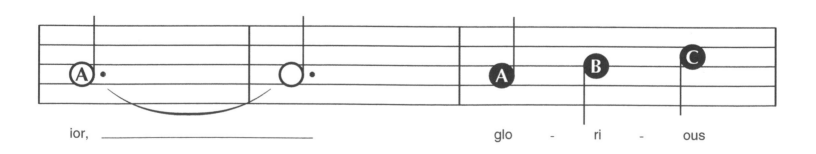

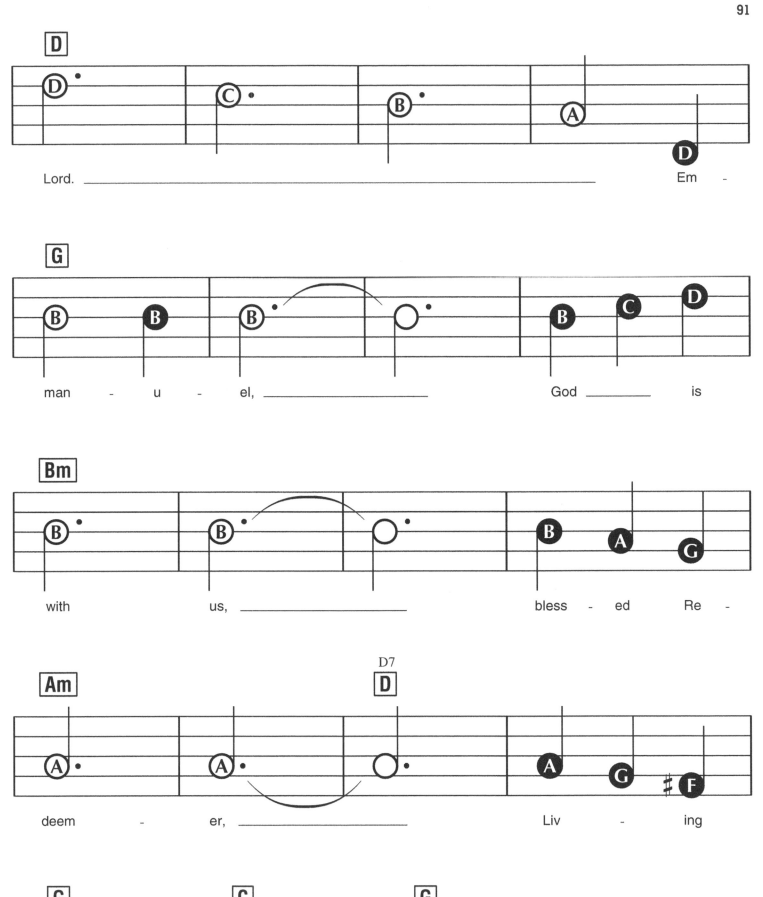

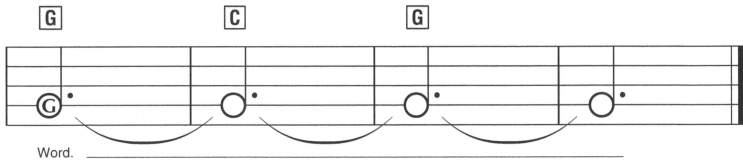

My Redeemer Lives

Registration 7
Rhythm: 16 Beat or Rock

Words and Music by
Reuben Morgan

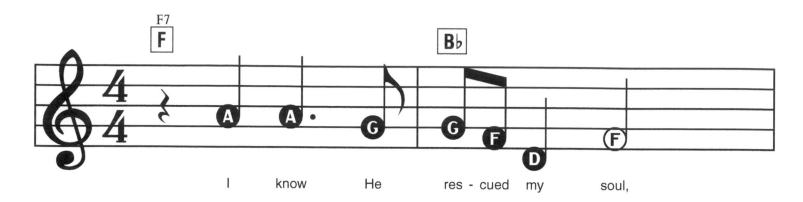

I know He res - cued my soul,

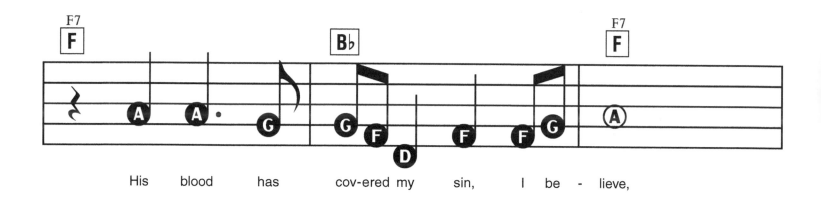

His blood has cov-ered my sin, I be - lieve,

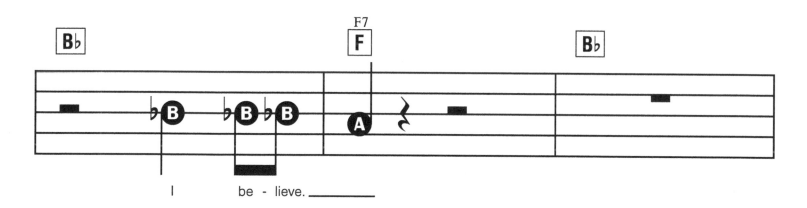

I be - lieve. _____

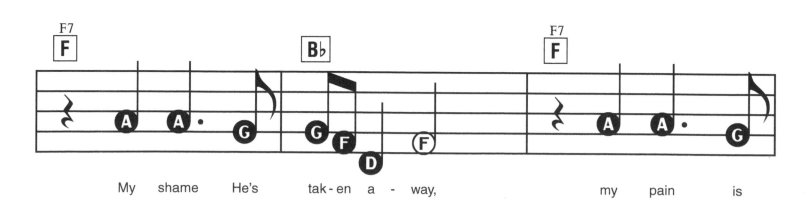

My shame He's tak-en a - way, my pain is

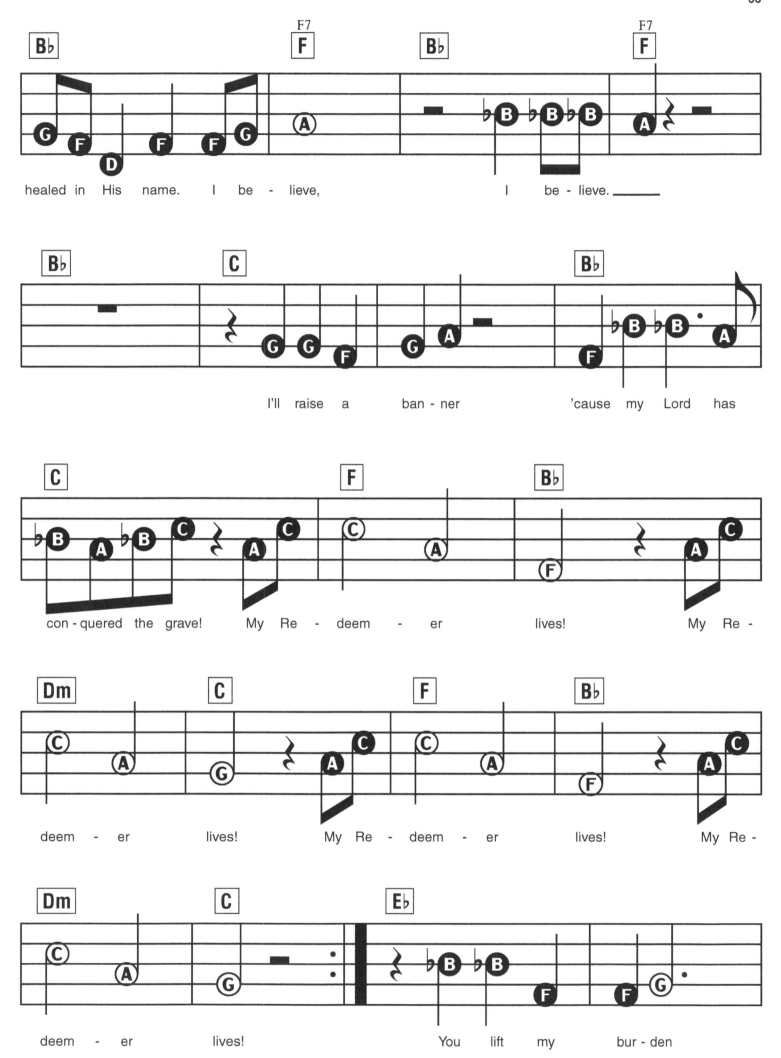

Lamb of God

Registration 1
Rhythm: Waltz

Words and Music by
Twila Paris

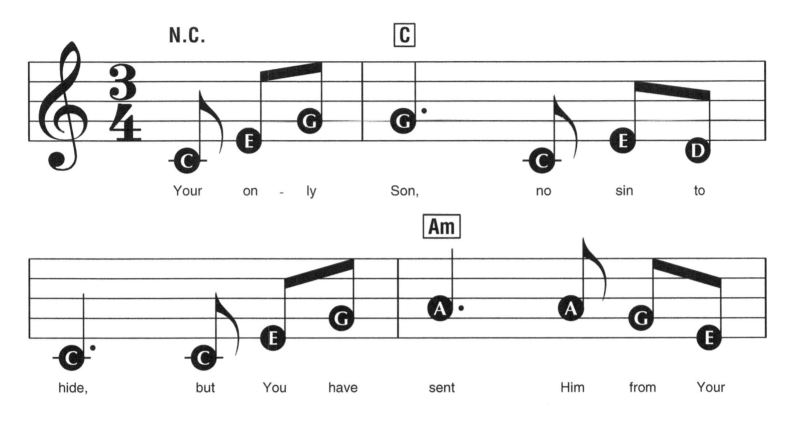

Your on - ly Son, no sin to

hide, but You have sent Him from Your

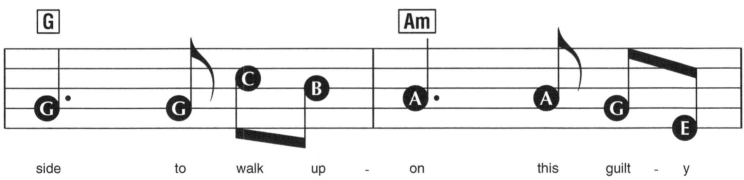

side to walk up - on this guilt - y

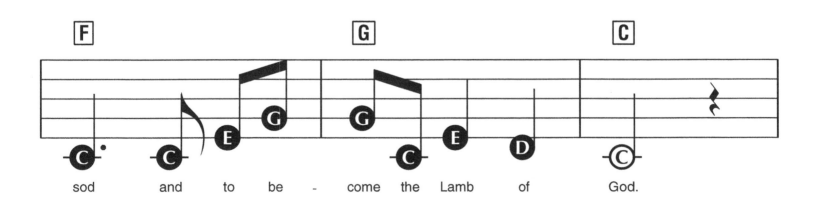

sod and to be - come the Lamb of God.

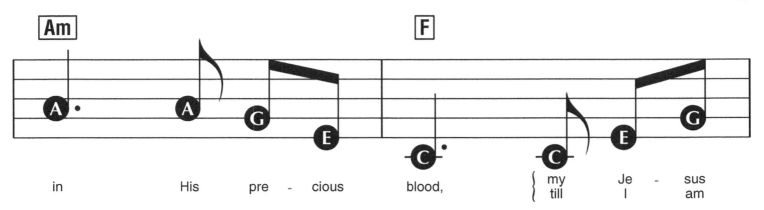

in His pre - cious blood, my Je - sus
till I am

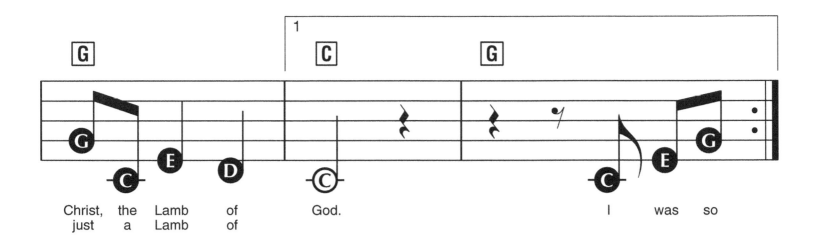

Christ, the Lamb of God. I was so
just a Lamb of

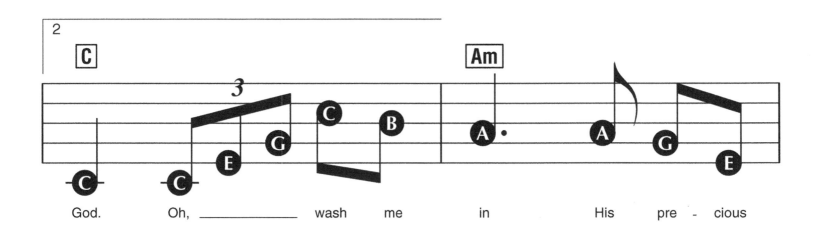

God. Oh, _____ wash me in His pre - cious

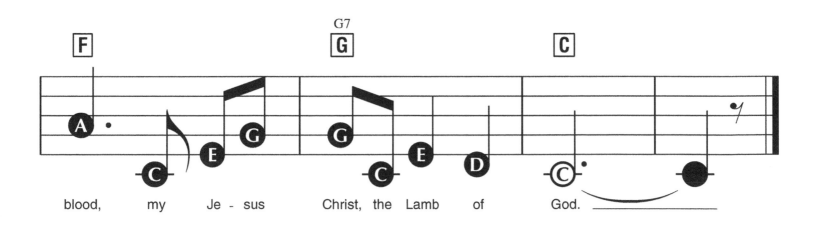

blood, my Je - sus Christ, the Lamb of God. _____

Lord, I Lift Your Name on High

Registration 7
Rhythm: Pop or 16 Beat

Words and Music by
Rick Founds

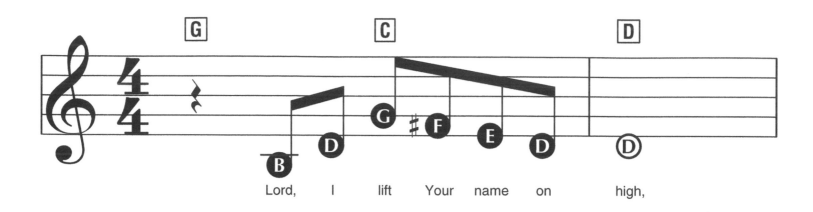

Lord, I lift Your name on high,

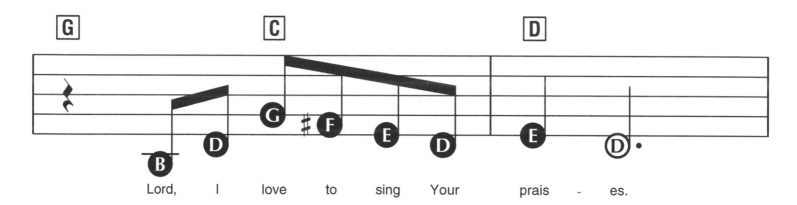

Lord, I love to sing Your prais - es.

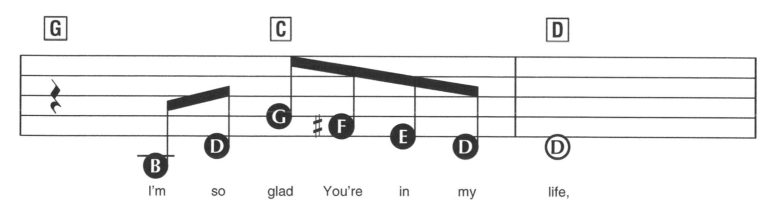

I'm so glad You're in my life,

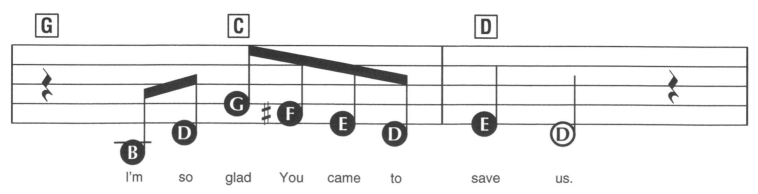

I'm so glad You came to save us.

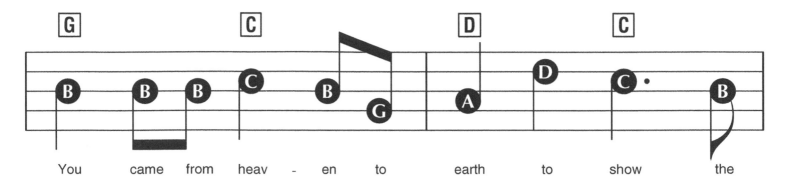

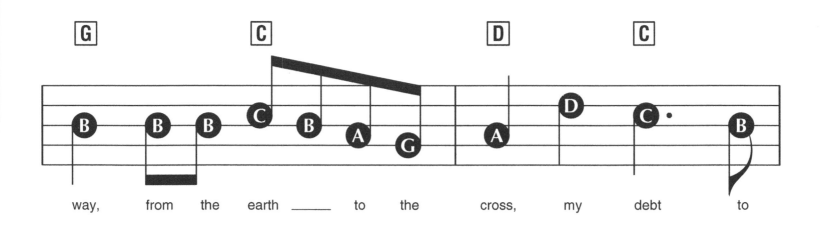

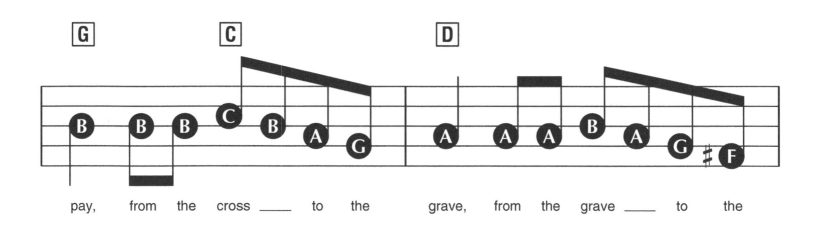

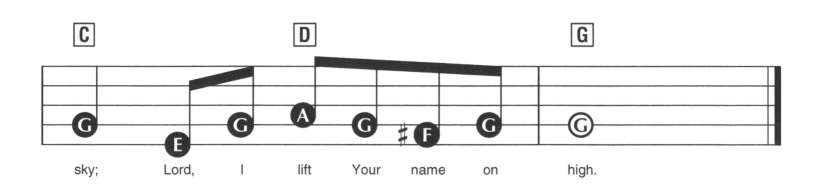

Lord, Reign in Me

Registration 8
Rhythm: Pop or 8 Beat

Words and Music by
Brenton Brown

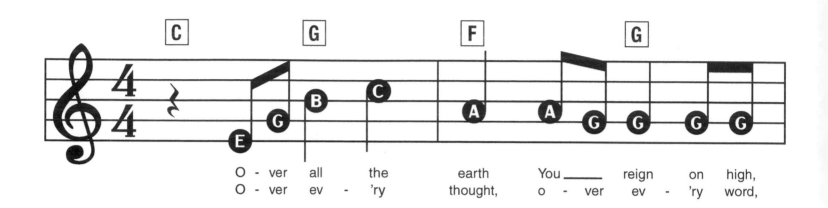

O - ver all the earth You ___ reign on high,
O - ver ev - 'ry thought, o - ver ev - 'ry word,

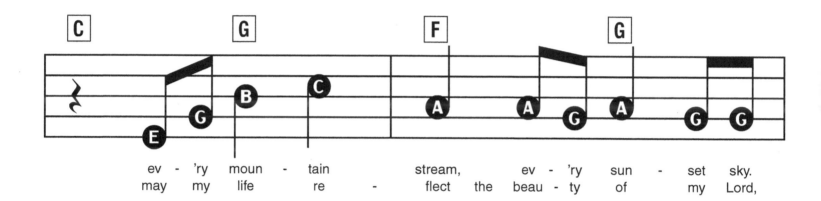

ev - 'ry moun - tain stream, ev - 'ry sun - set sky.
may my life re - flect the beau - ty of my Lord,

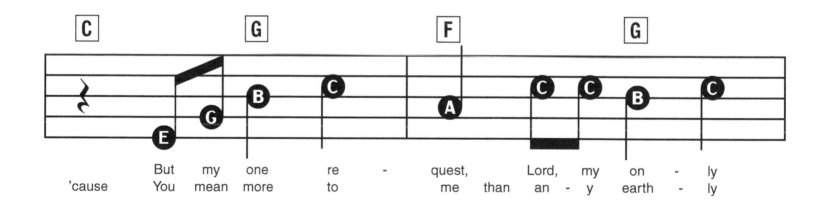

But my one re - quest, Lord, my on - ly
'cause You mean more to me than an - y earth - ly

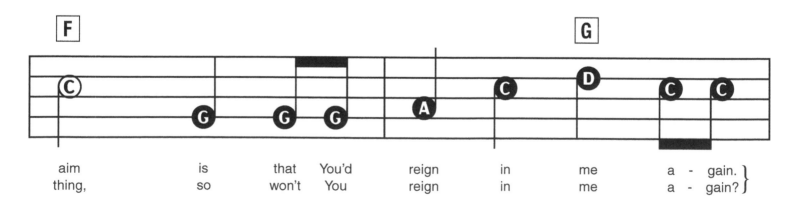

aim is that You'd reign in me a - gain.
thing, so won't You reign in me a - gain?

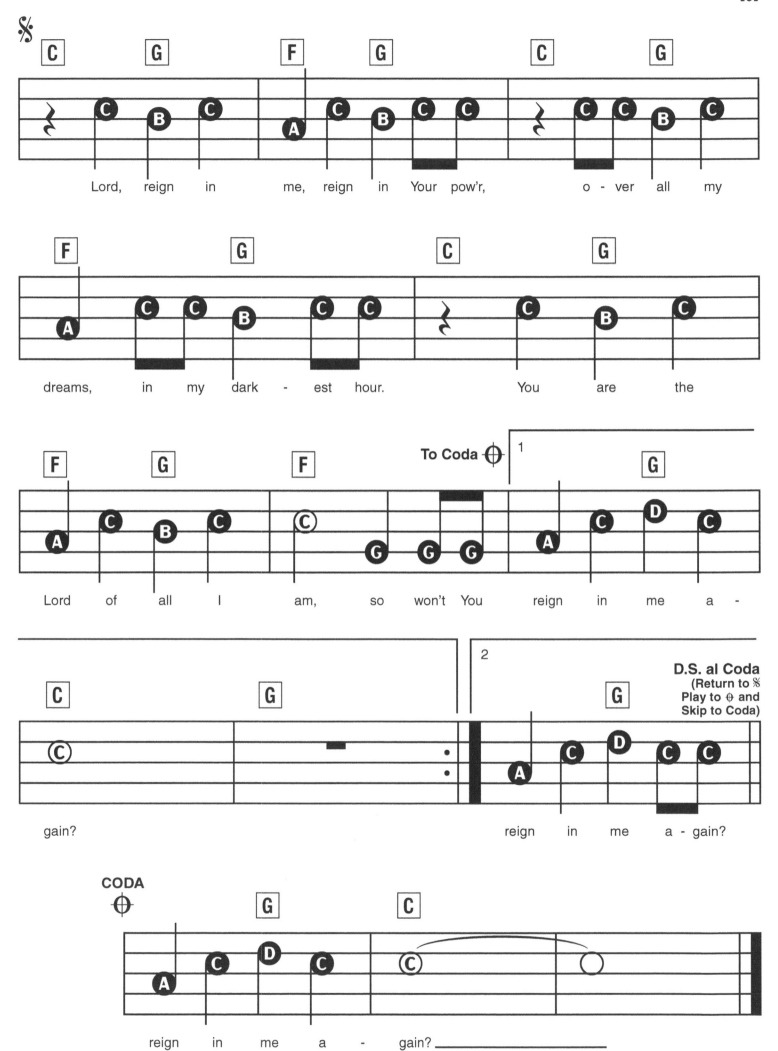

Majesty

Registration 2
Rhythm: March or 8 Beat

Words and Music by
Jack W. Hayford

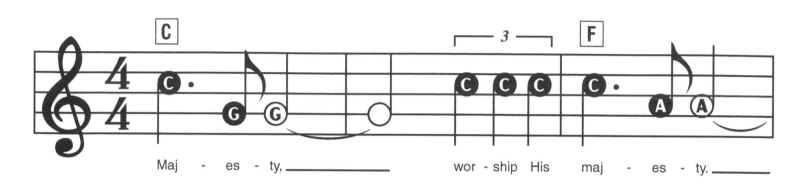

Maj - es - ty, _____ wor - ship His maj - es - ty. _____

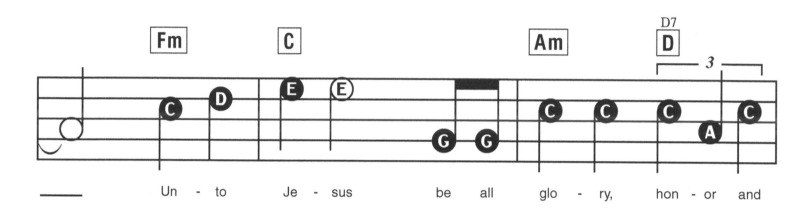

_____ Un - to Je - sus be all glo - ry, hon - or and

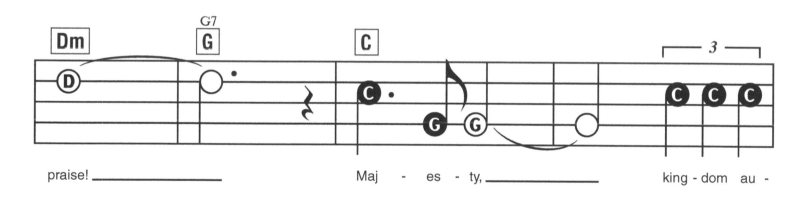

praise! _____ Maj - es - ty, _____ king - dom au -

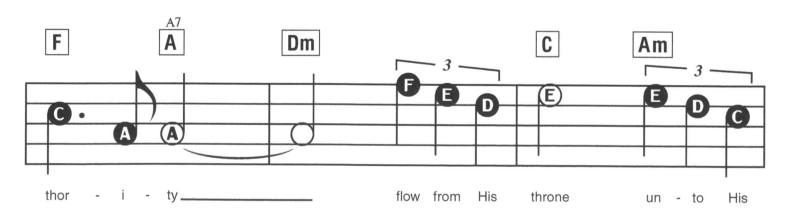

thor - i - ty _____ flow from His throne un - to His

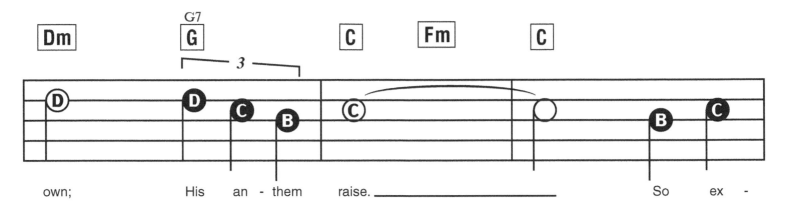

own; His an - them raise. _____ So ex -

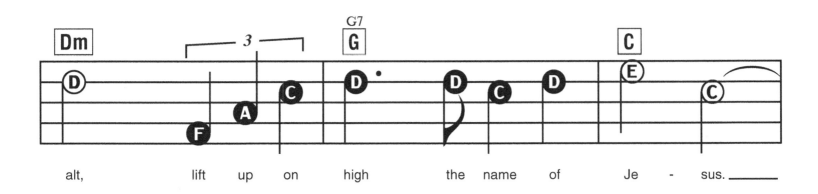

alt, lift up on high the name of Je - sus. _____

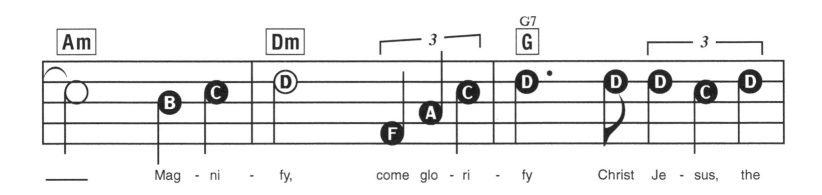

_____ Mag - ni - fy, come glo - ri - fy Christ Je - sus, the

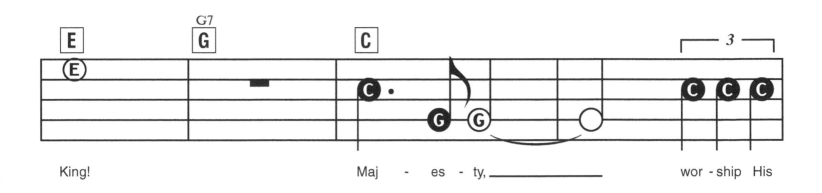

King! Maj - es - ty, _____ wor - ship His

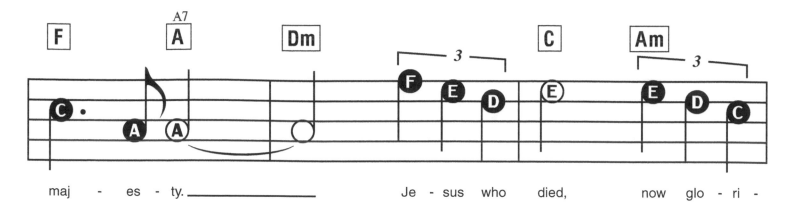

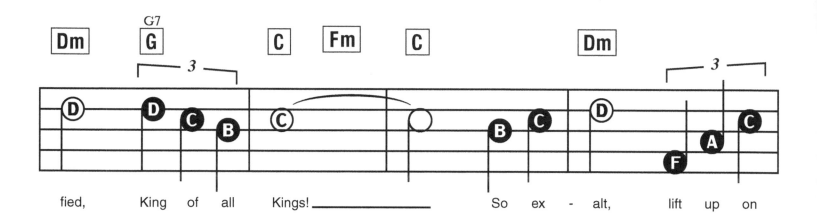

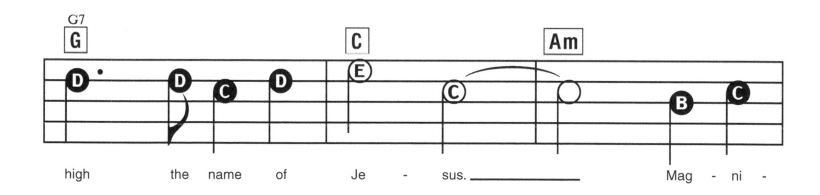

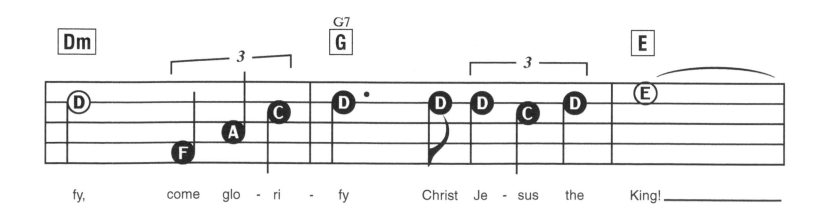

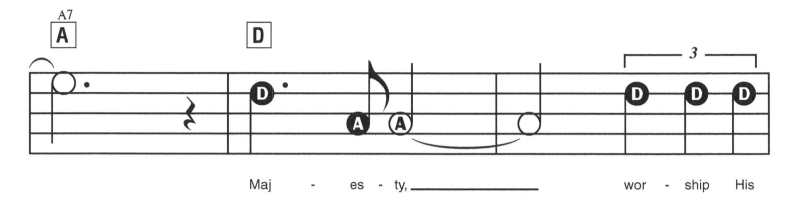

Maj - es - ty, _____ wor - ship His

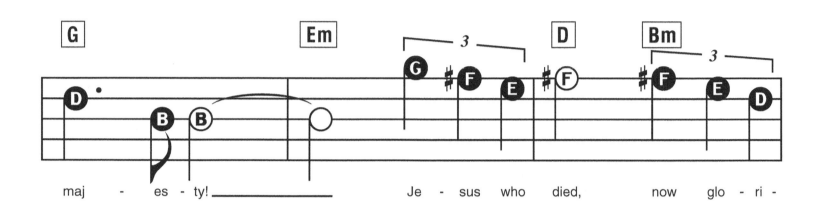

maj - es - ty! _____ Je - sus who died, now glo - ri -

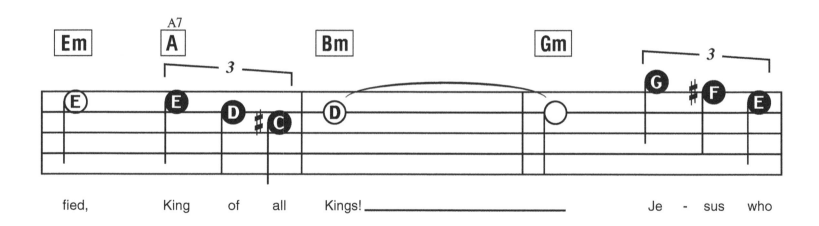

fied, King of all Kings! _____ Je - sus who

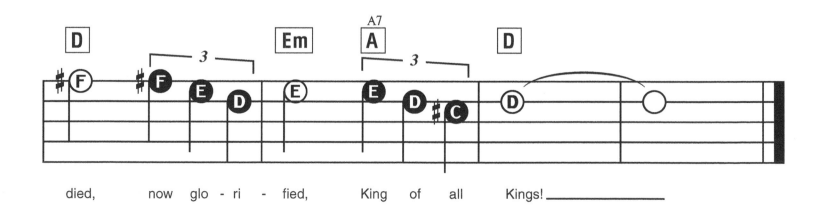

died, now glo - ri - fied, King of all Kings! _____

Mighty Is Our God

Registration 7
Rhythm: 8 Beat or Rock

Words and Music by Eugene Greco,
Gerrit Gustafson and Don Moen

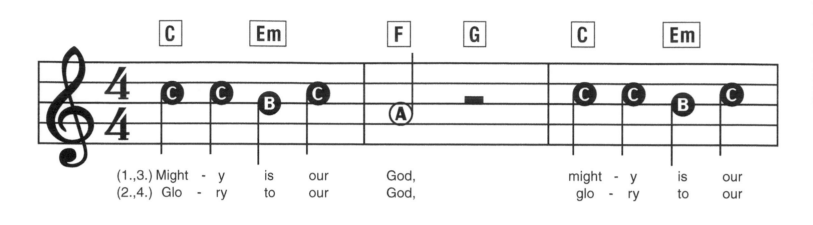

(1.,3.) Might - y is our God, might - y is our
(2.,4.) Glo - ry to our God, glo - ry to our

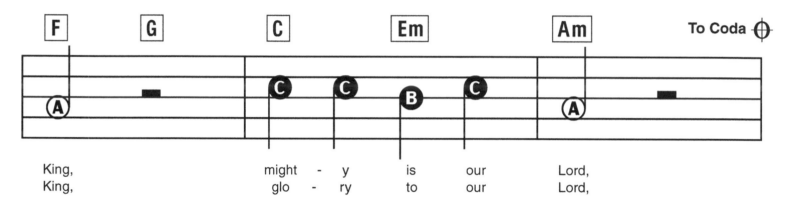

King, might - y is our Lord,
King, glo - ry to our Lord,

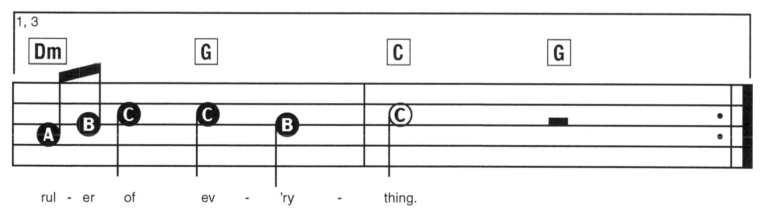

rul - er of ev - 'ry - thing.

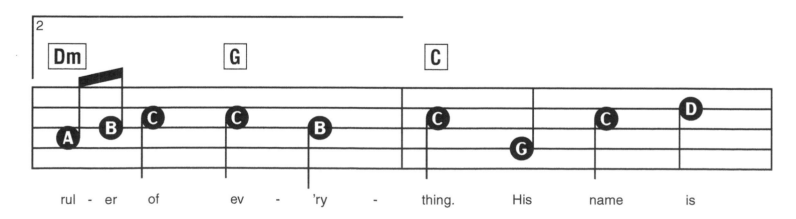

rul - er of ev - 'ry - thing. His name is

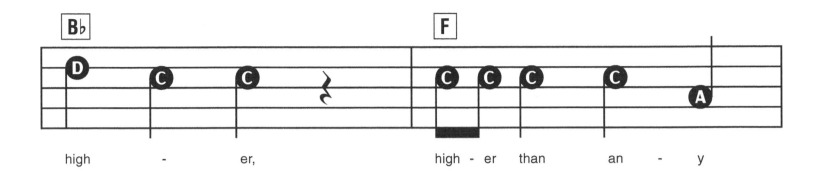

high - er, high-er than an - y

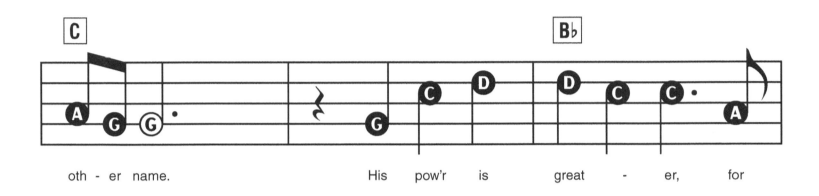

oth - er name. His pow'r is great - er, for

D.C. al Coda
G7 (Return to beginning
Play to ⊕ and
Skip to Coda)

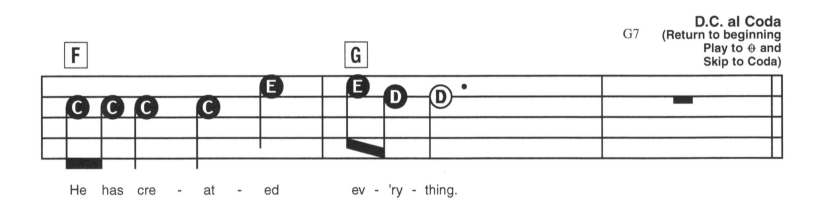

He has cre - at - ed ev - 'ry - thing.

CODA

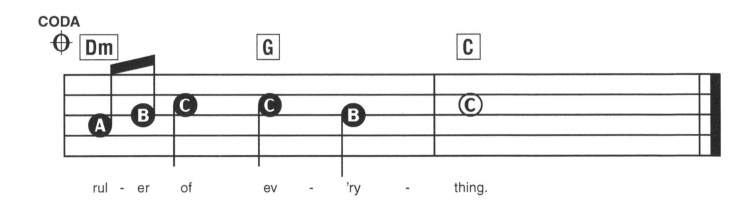

rul - er of ev - 'ry - thing.

More Love, More Power

Registration 2
Rhythm: 8 Beat or Rock

Words and Music by
Jude Del Hierro

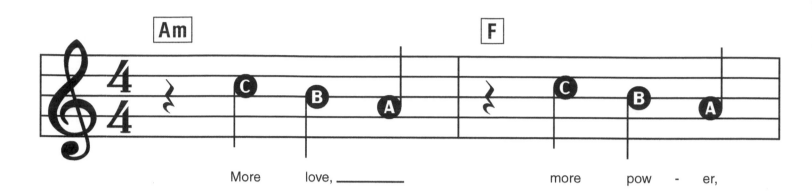

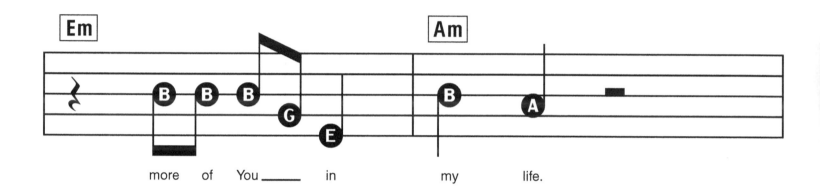

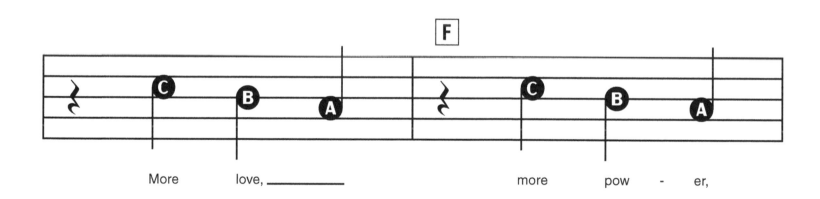

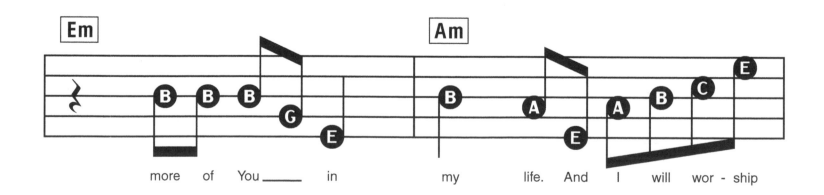

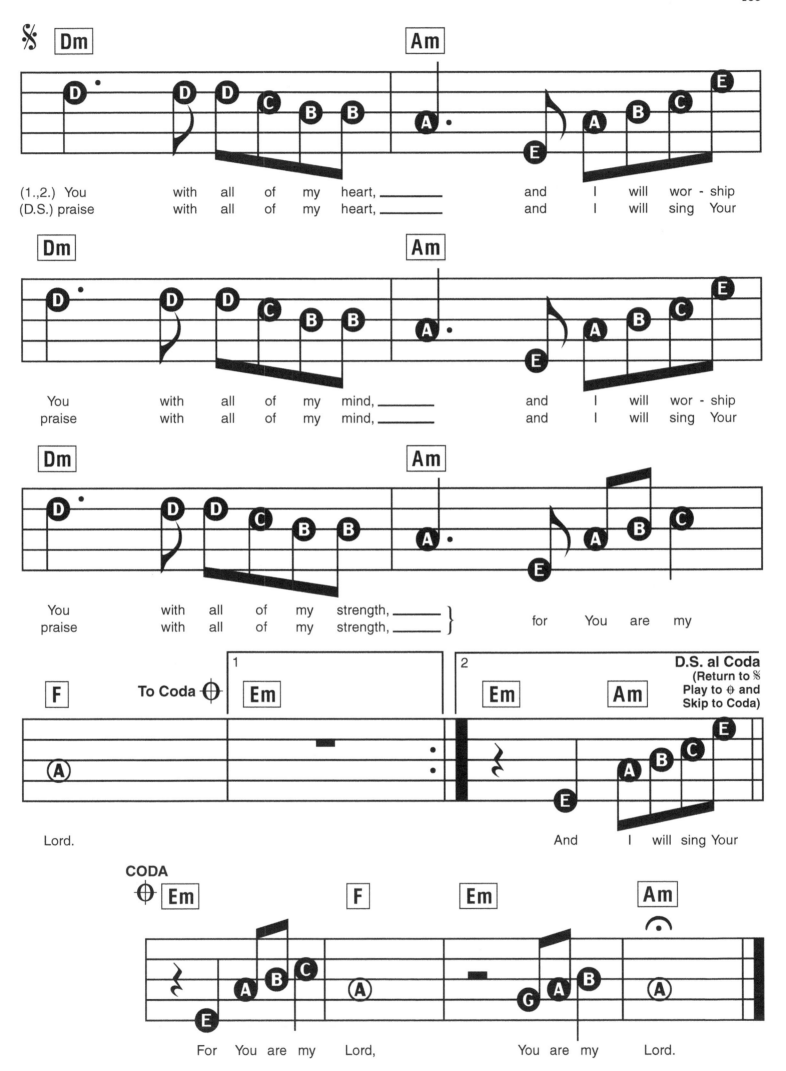

More Precious Than Silver

Registration 1
Rhythm: Ballad

Words and Music by
Lynn DeShazo

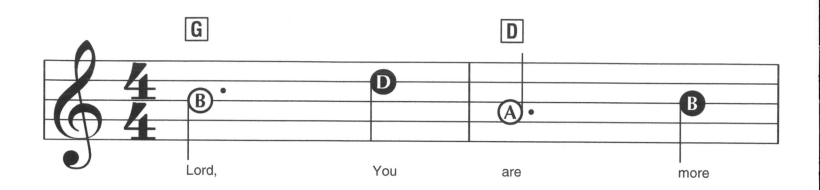

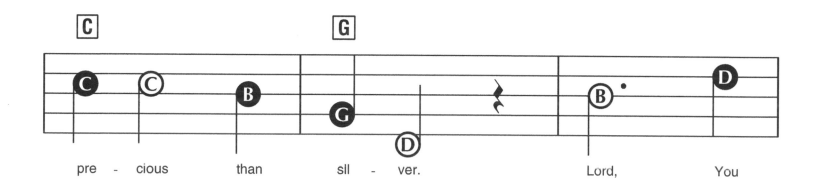

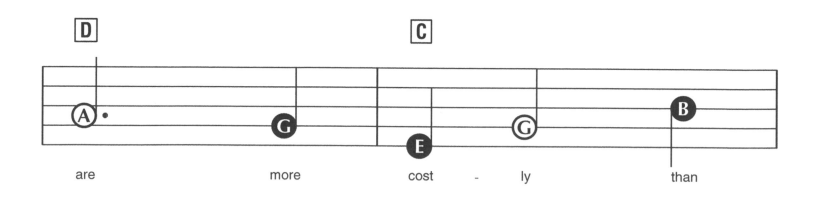

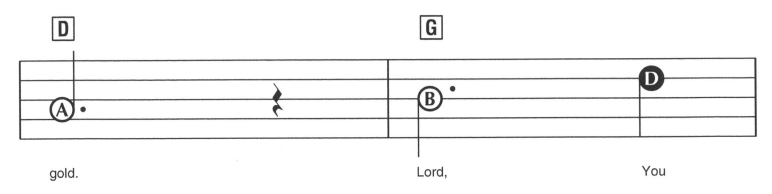

gold.　　　　　　　　　　Lord,　　　　　　　You

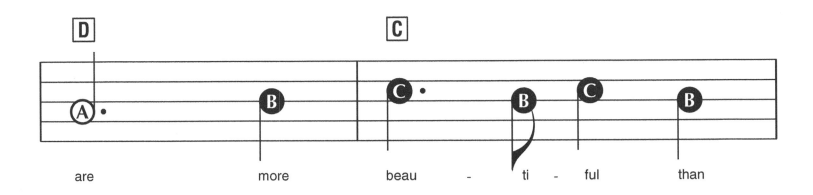

are　　　　more　　beau　-　ti　-　ful　than

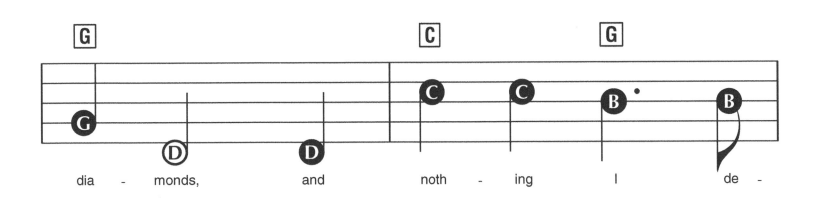

dia　-　monds,　　and　　noth　-　ing　I　　de　-

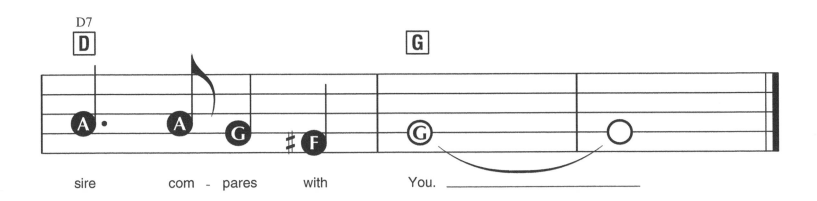

sire　　com　-　pares　with　　You. _____

My Life Is in You, Lord

Registration 7
Rhythm: 8 Beat or Rock

Words and Music by
Daniel Gardner

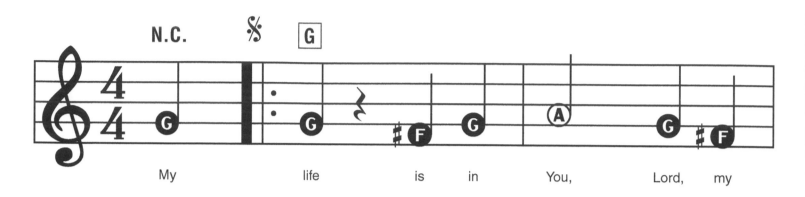

My life is in You, Lord, my

strength is in You, Lord, my hope is in

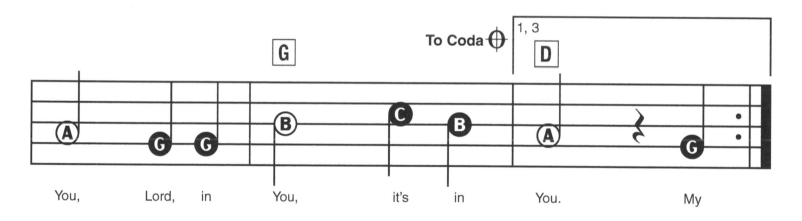

You, Lord, in You, it's in You. My

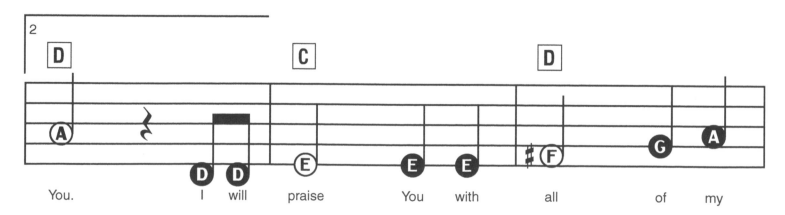

You. I will praise You with all of my

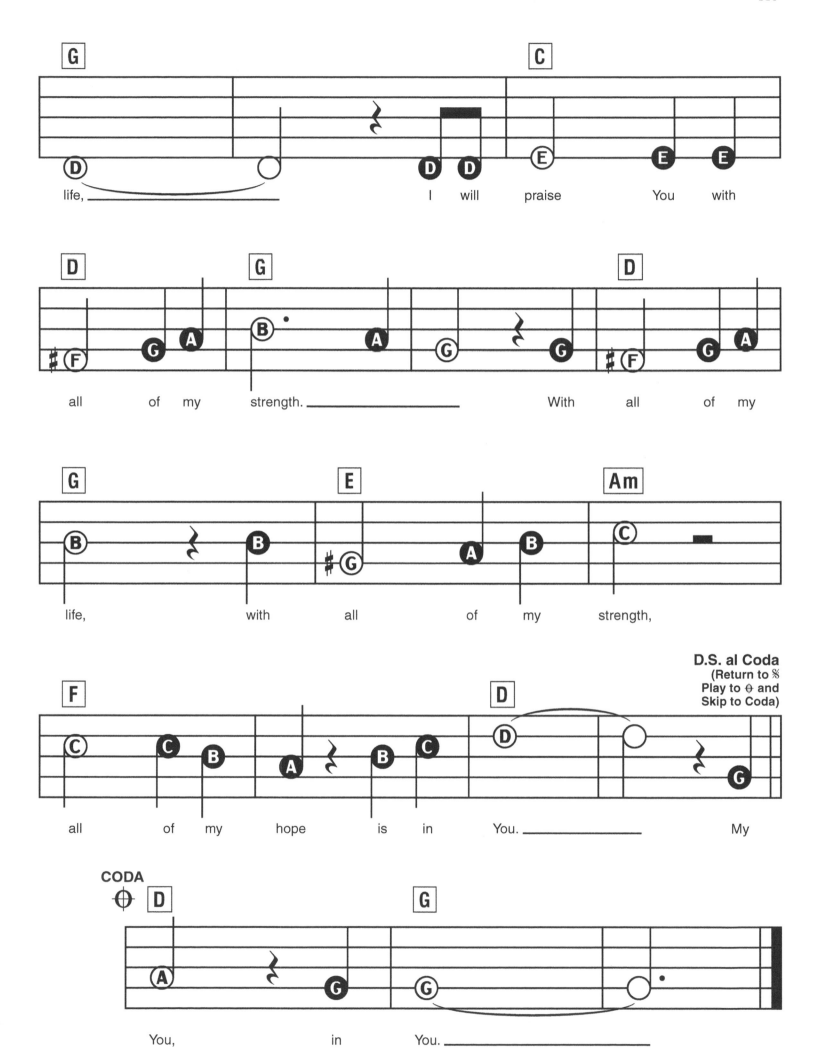

Oh Lord, You're Beautiful

Registration 3
Rhythm: Ballad

Words and Music by
Keith Green

N.C.

| Oh | (1.,2.) Lord, | You're | beau | - ti | - |
| | (3.) Lord, | please | light | the | ___ |

G　**C**　**G**

D　　D7　　**G**

| ful. | | Your | face | is |
| fire | | that | once | burned |

C　**G**　**D**

| all | I | seek, | for |
| bright | and | clear. | Re - |

Em　**B**　**Em**　**D**

| when | Your ___ | eyes | are | on | this |
| place | the ___ | lamp | of | my | first |

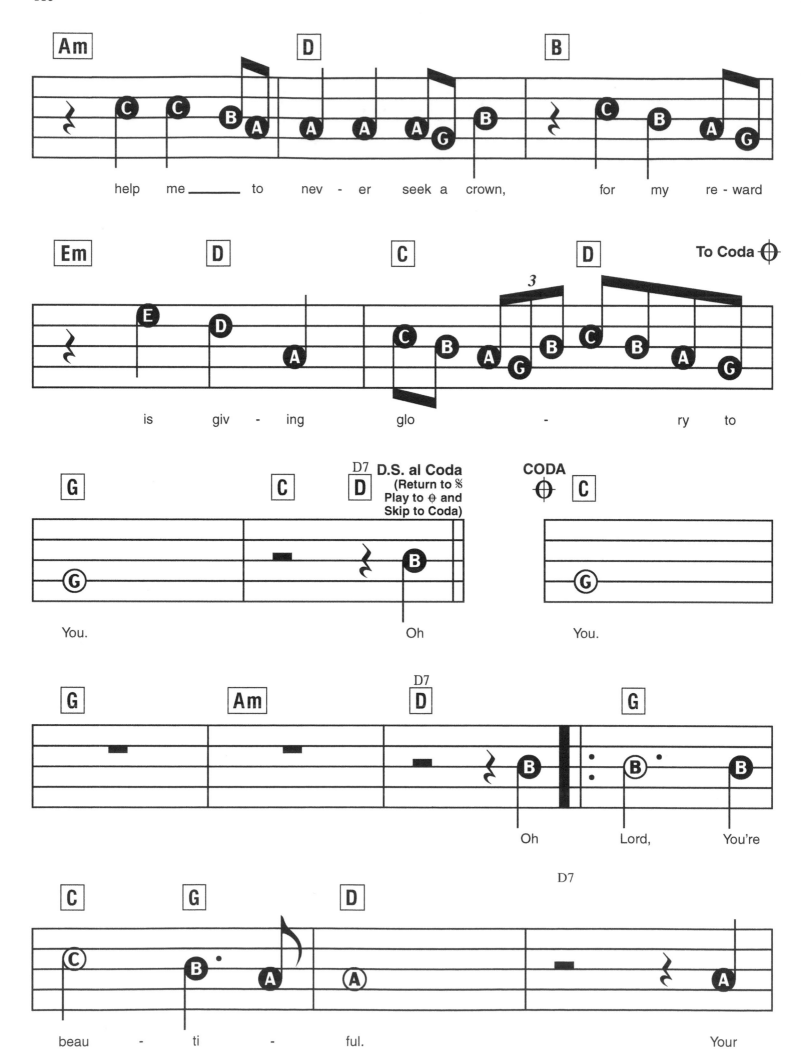

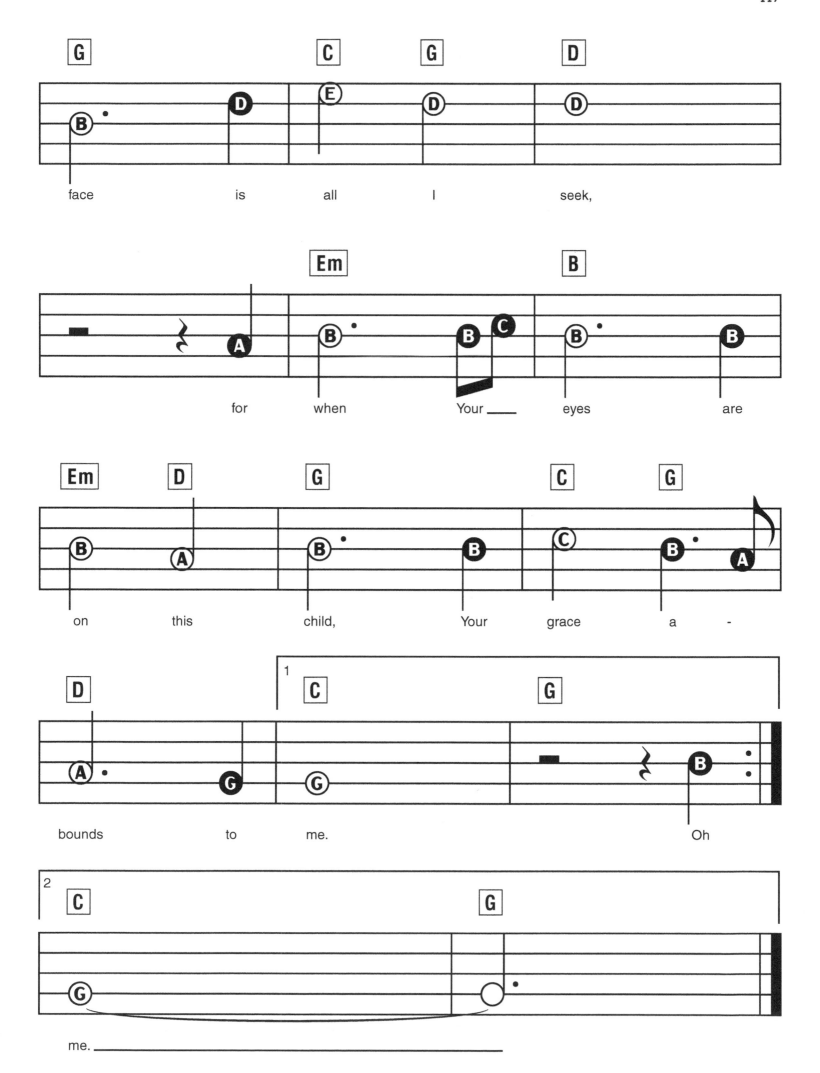

Open the Eyes of My Heart

Registration 8
Rhythm: 8 Beat or Rock

Words and Music by
Paul Baloche

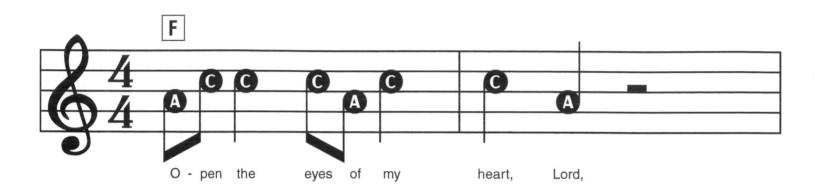

O - pen the eyes of my heart, Lord,

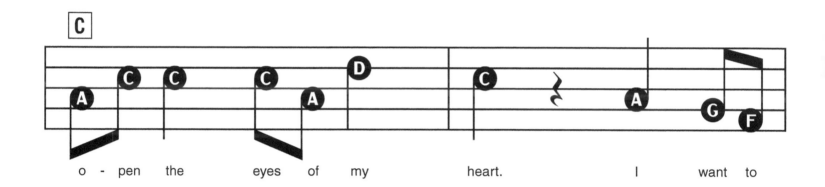

o - pen the eyes of my heart. I want to

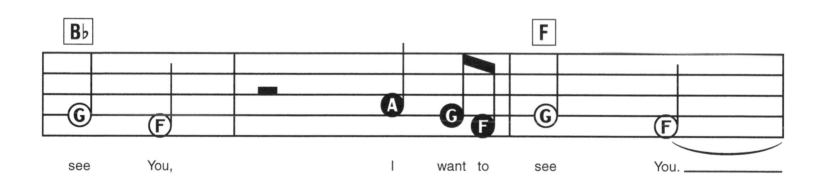

see You, I want to see You. _____

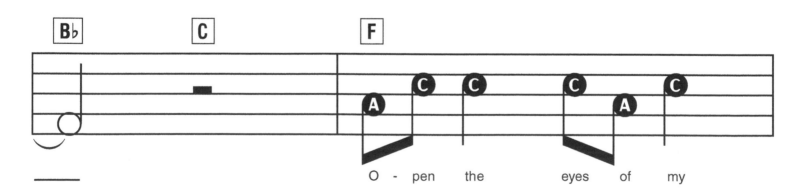

_____ O - pen the eyes of my

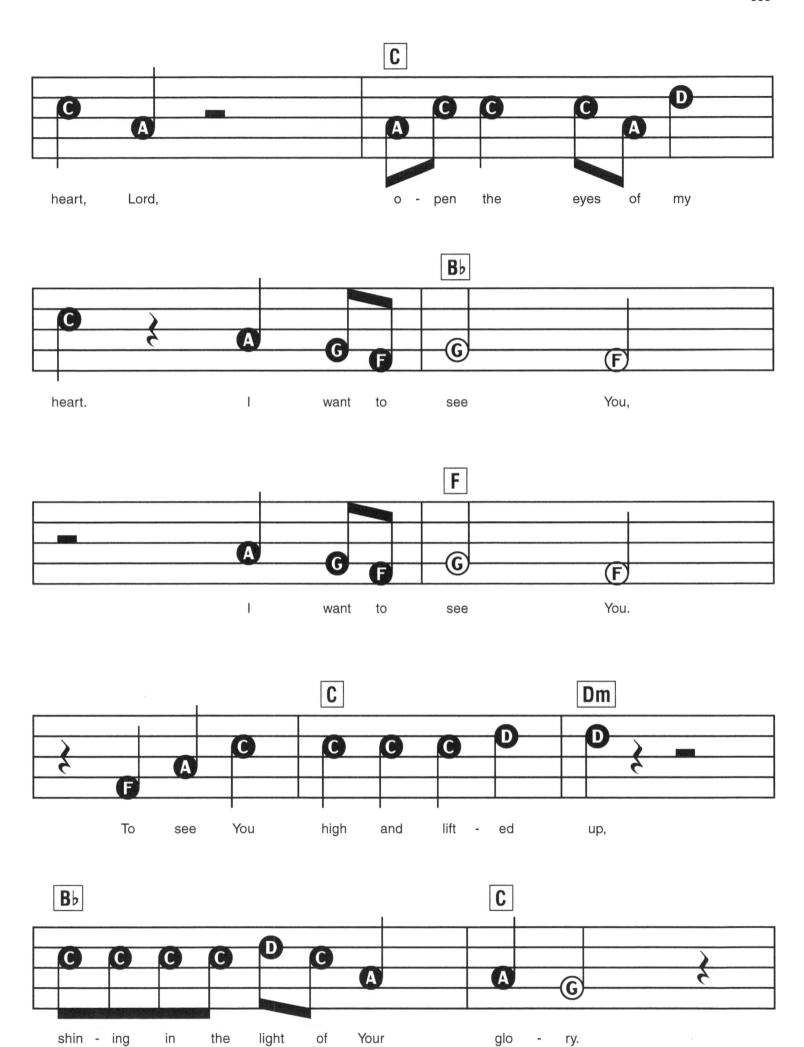

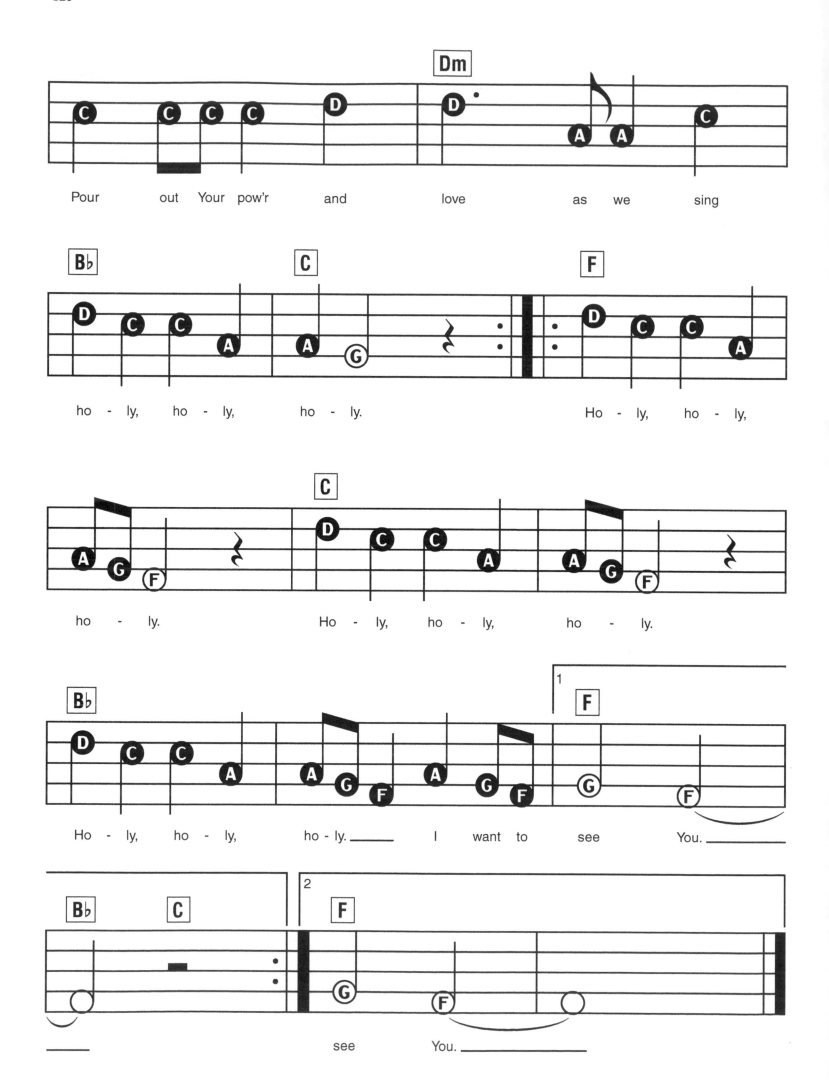

The Potter's Hand

Registration 1
Rhythm: Ballad or 8 Beat

Words and Music by
Darlene Zschech

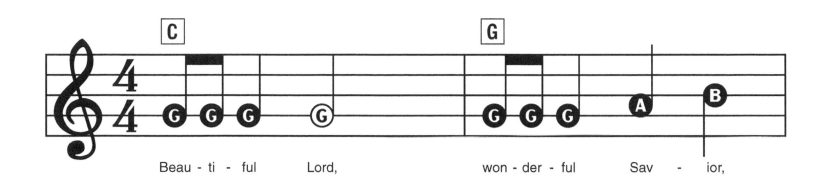

Beau - ti - ful   Lord,   won - der - ful   Sav - ior,

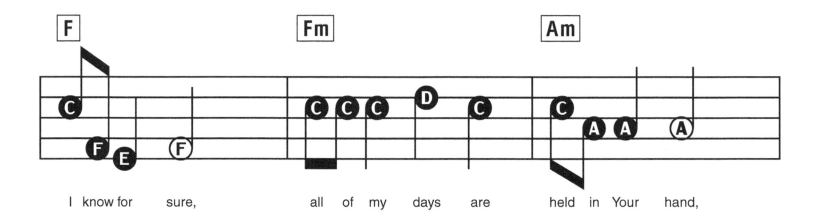

I know for   sure,   all of my days are   held in Your hand,

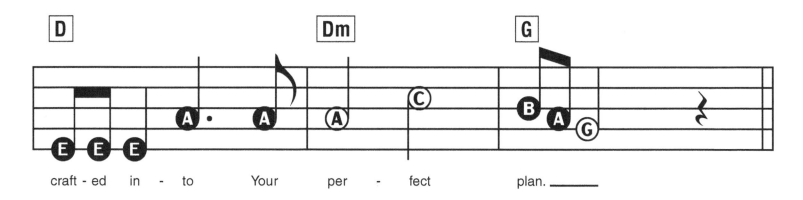

craft - ed in - to   Your   per - fect   plan. _____

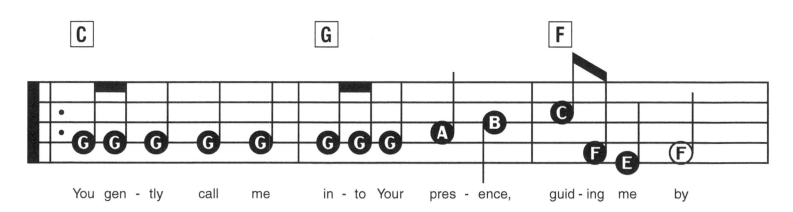

You gen - tly   call   me   in - to Your pres - ence,   guid - ing me   by

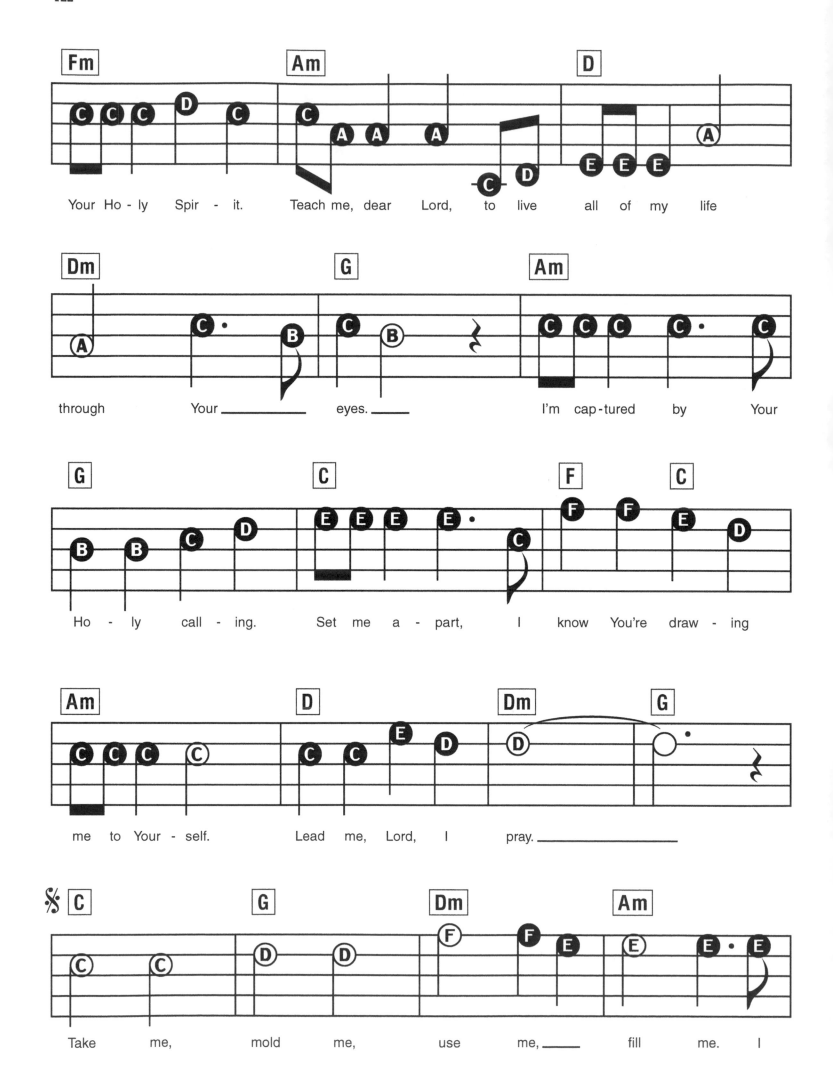

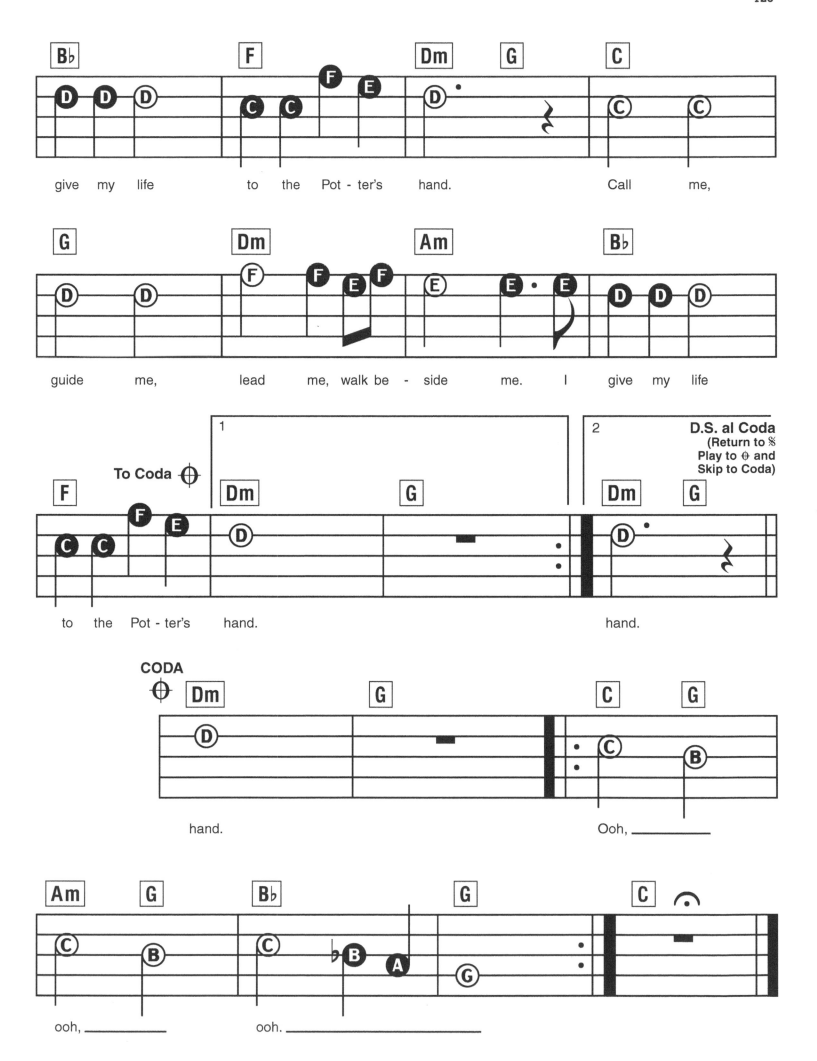

Shine, Jesus, Shine

Registration 2
Rhythm: 16 Beat or Disco

Words and Music by
Graham Kendrick

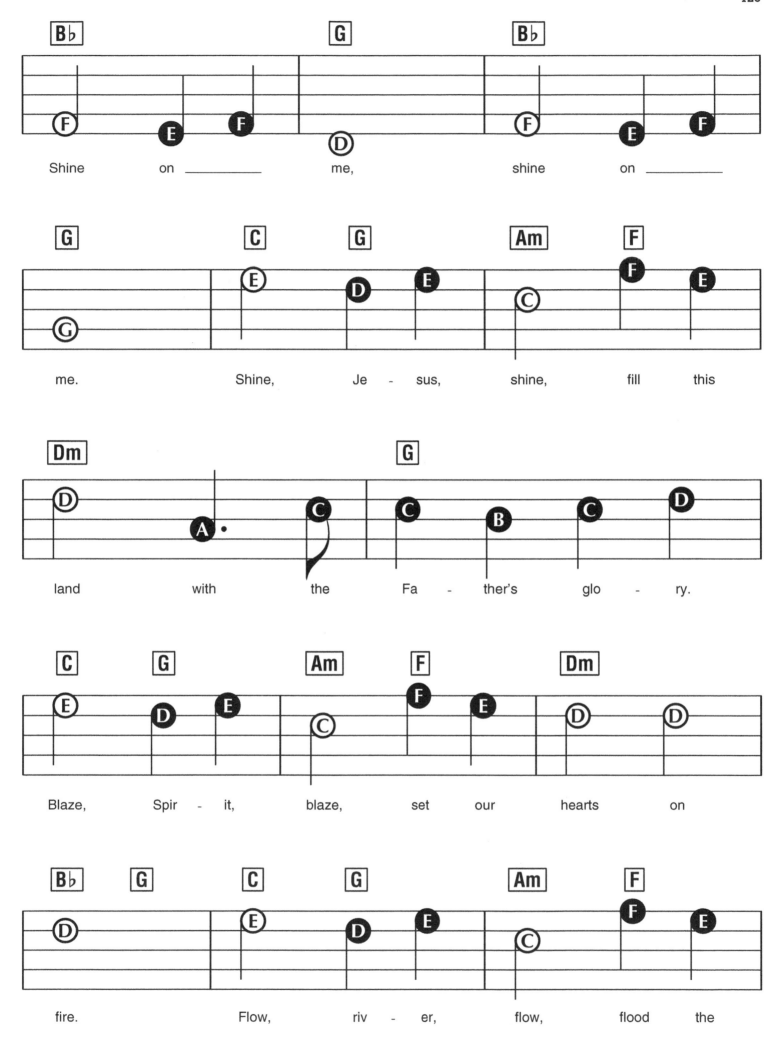

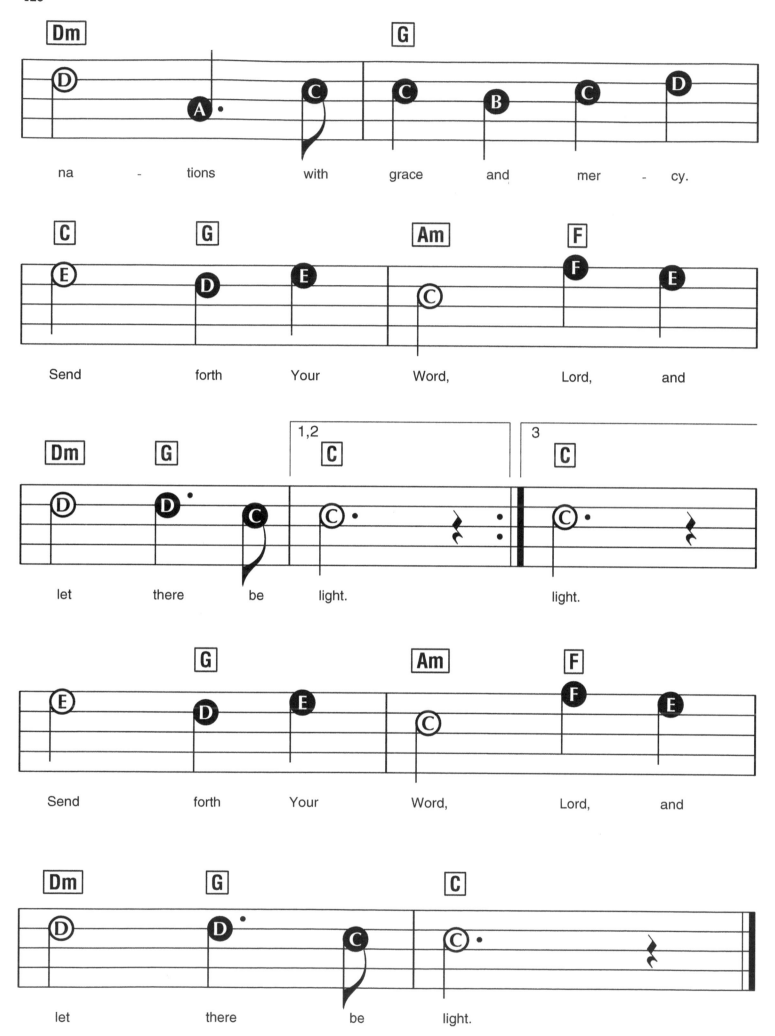

Shout to the Lord

Registration 2
Rhythm: Ballad or 8 Beat

Words and Music by
Darlene Zschech

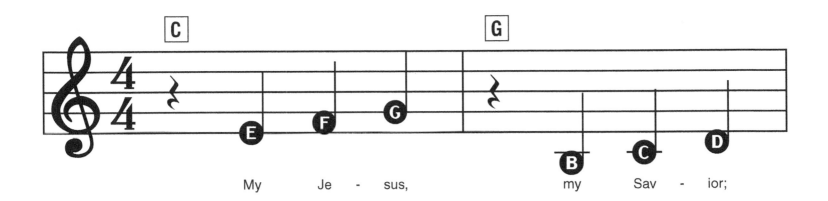

My Je - sus, my Sav - ior;

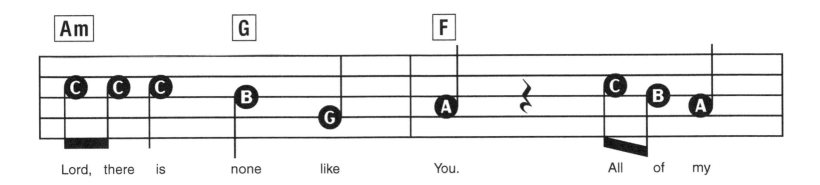

Lord, there is none like You. All of my

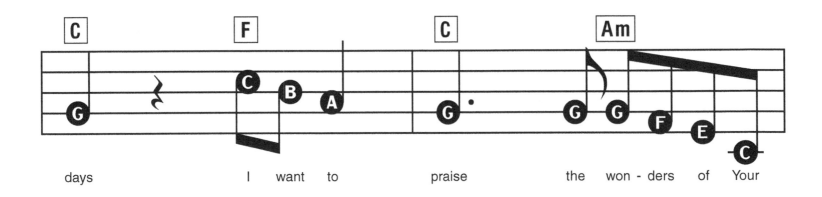

days I want to praise the won - ders of Your

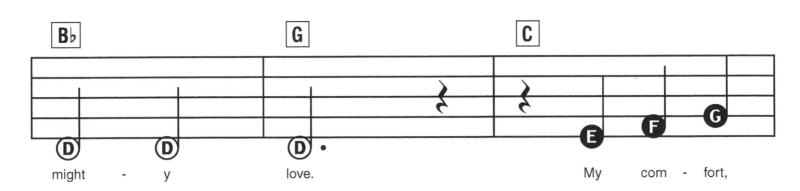

might - y love. My com - fort,

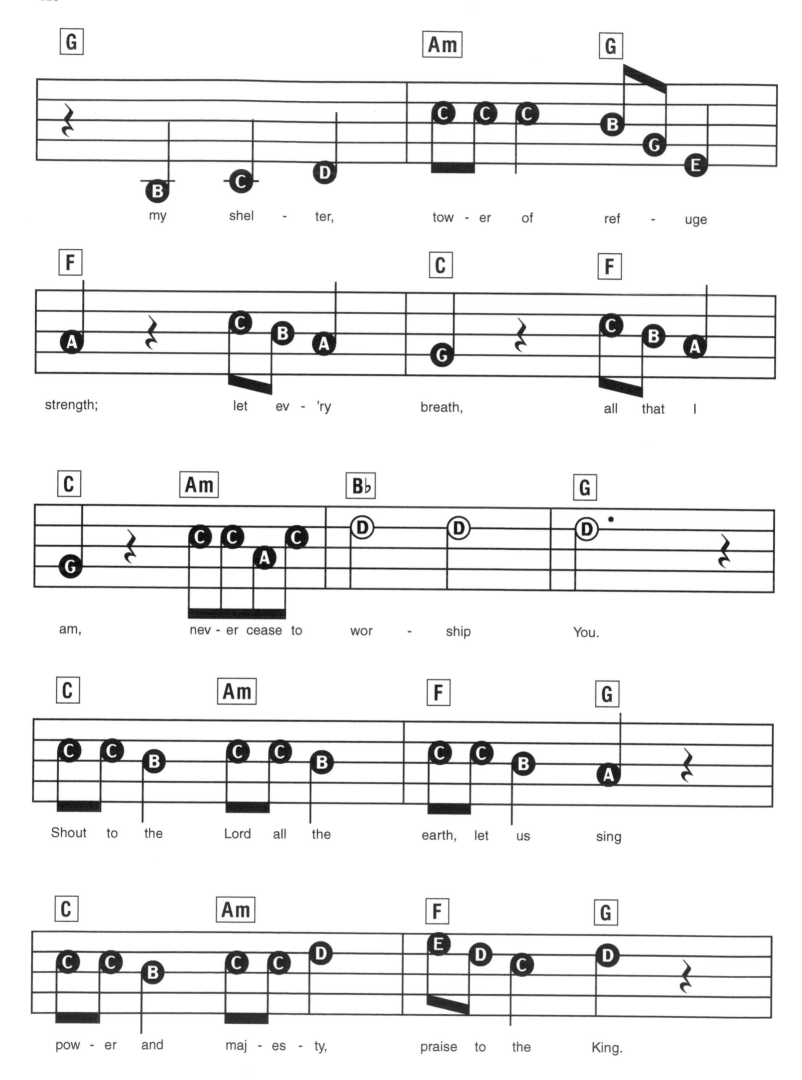

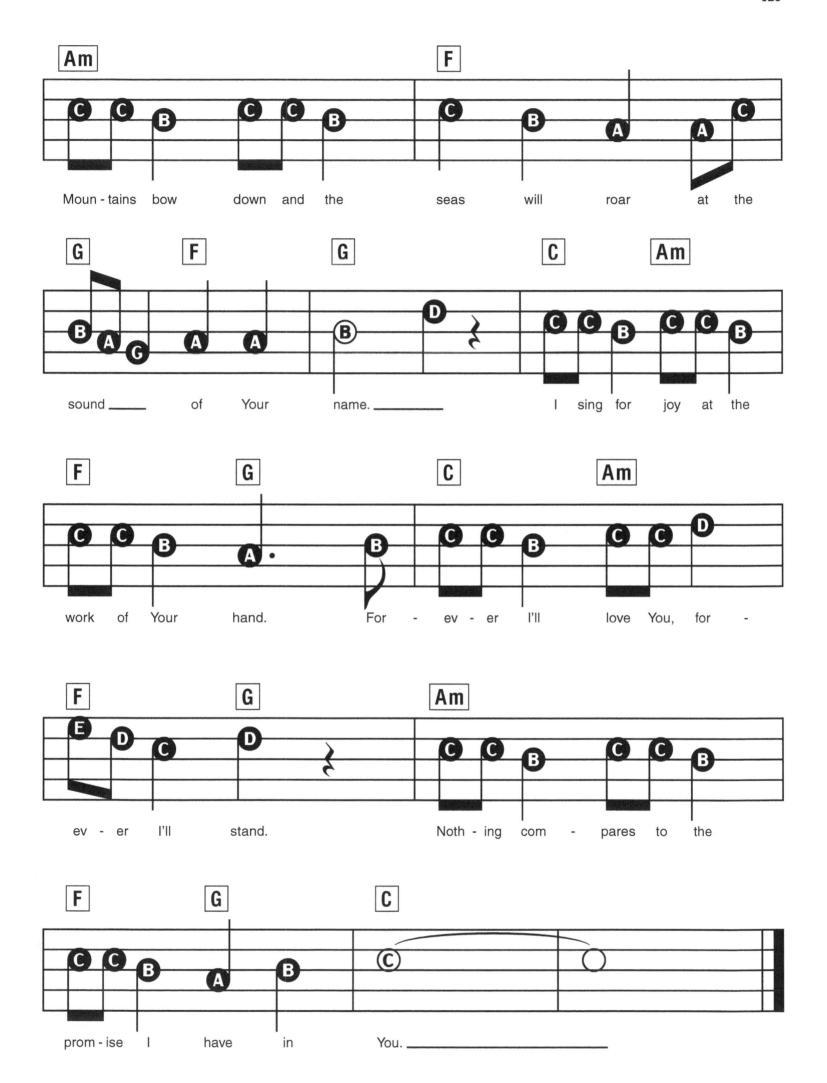

Shine on Us

Registration 3
Rhythm: Ballad

Words and Music by Michael W. Smith
and Debbie Smith

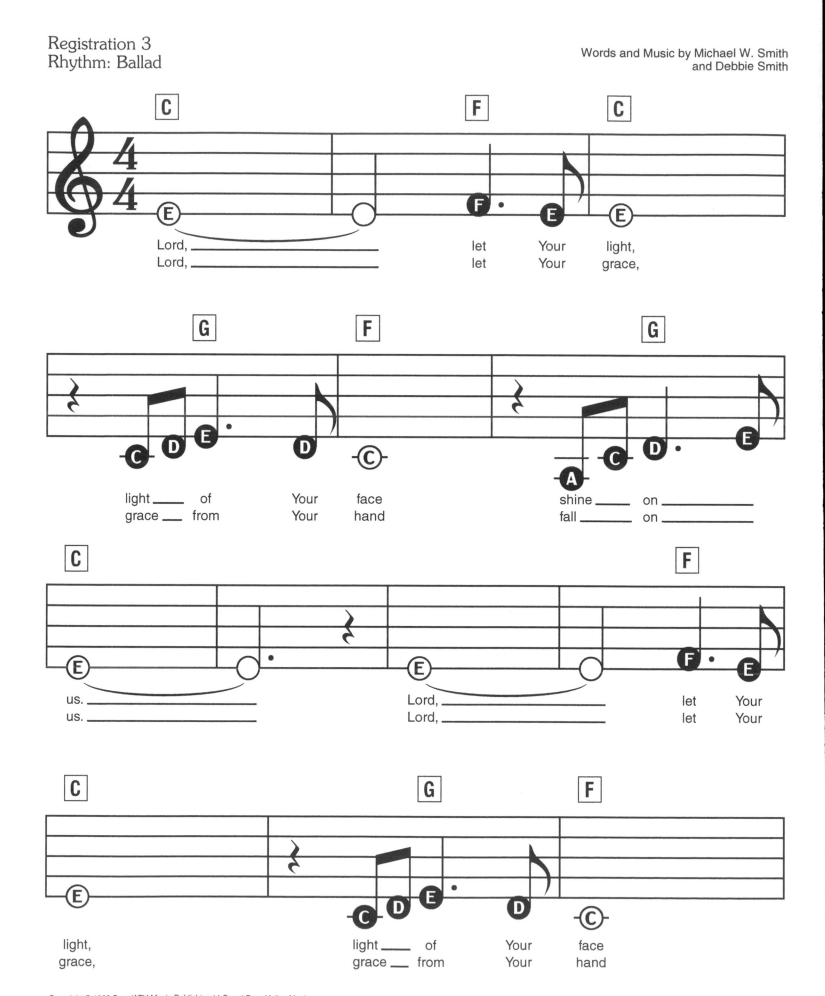

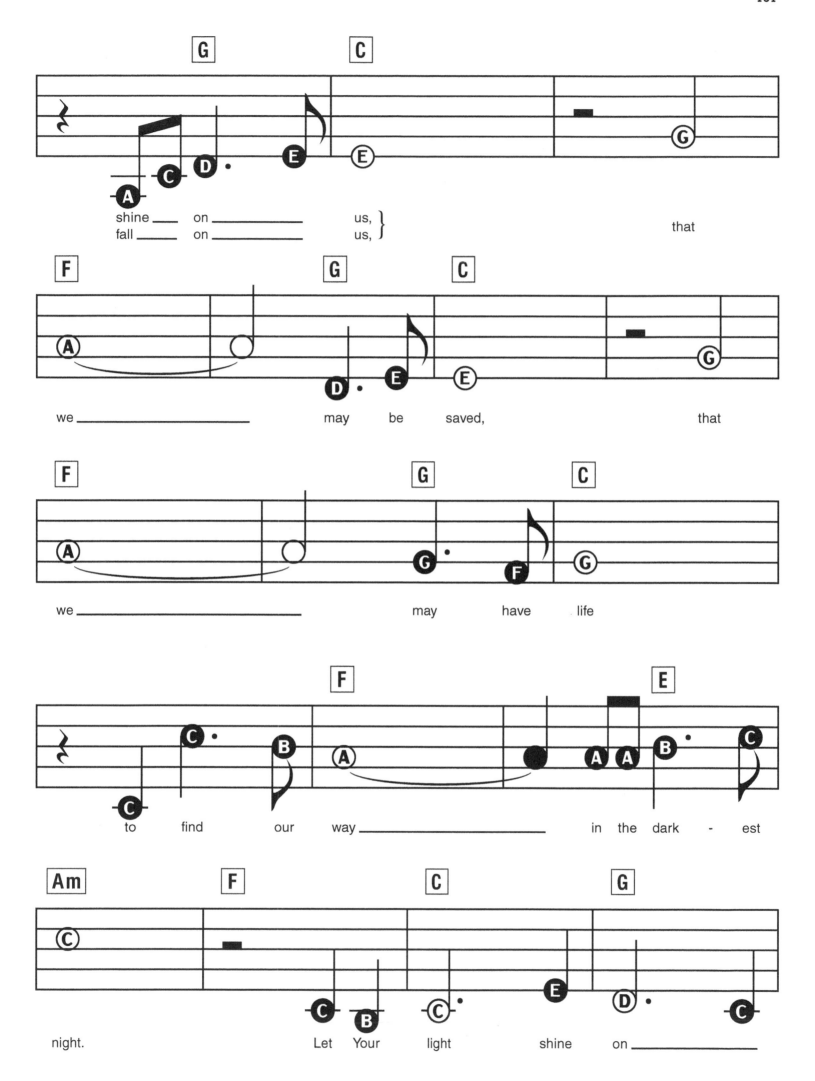

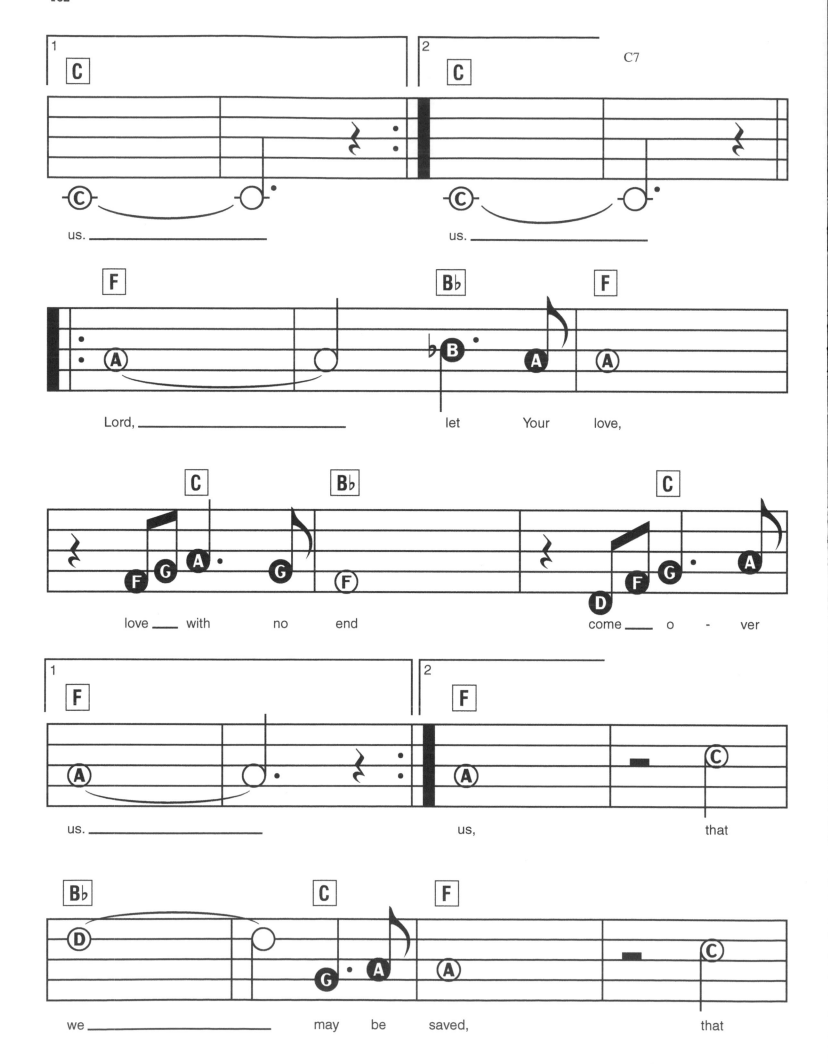

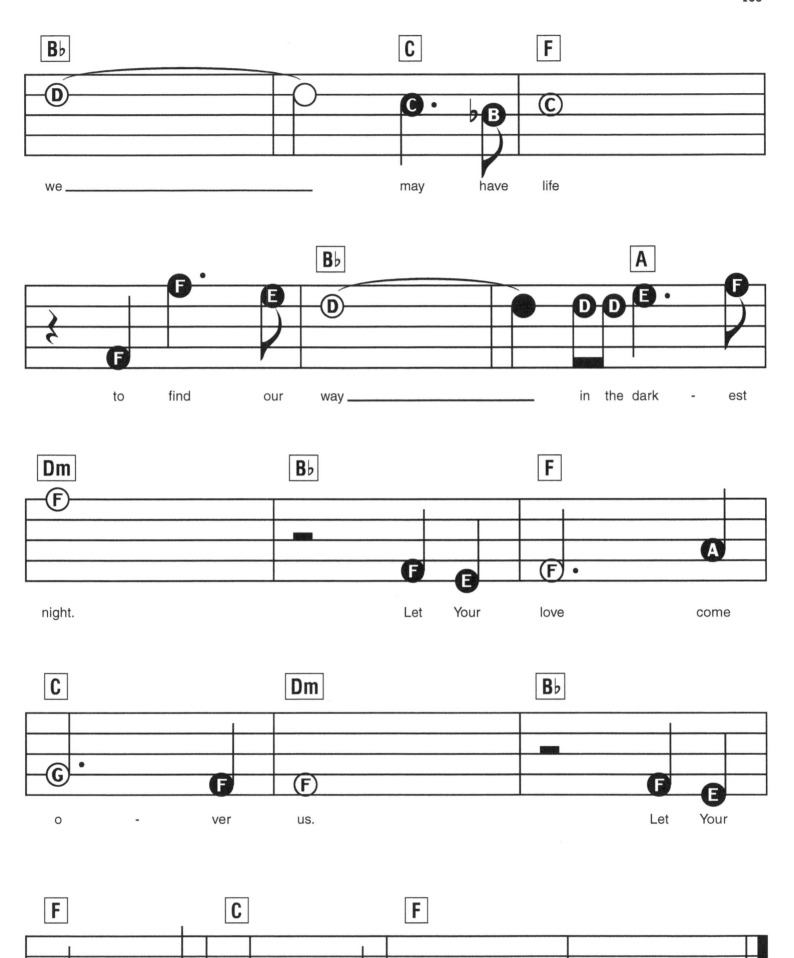

Step by Step

Registration 4
Rhythm: 8 Beat or Ballad

Words and Music by
David Strasser "Beaker"

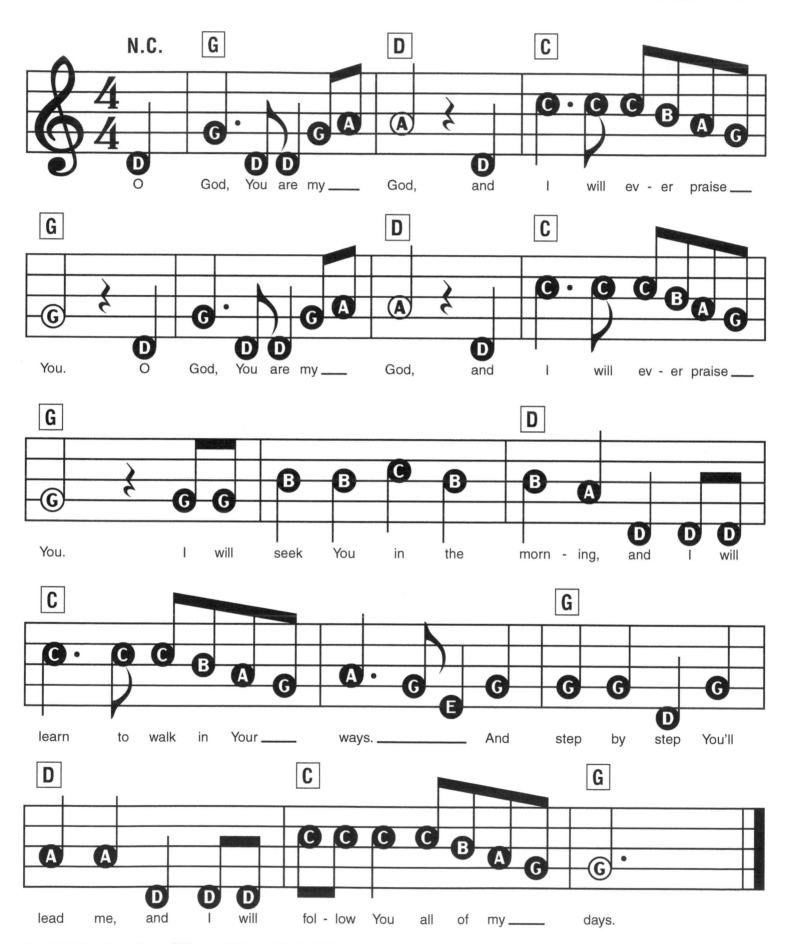

There Is None Like You

Registration 8
Rhythm: Ballad or 8 Beat

Words and Music by
Lenny LeBlanc

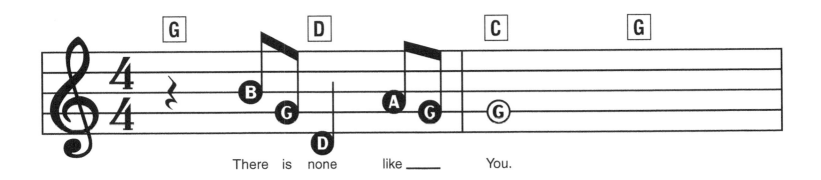

There is none like ____ You.

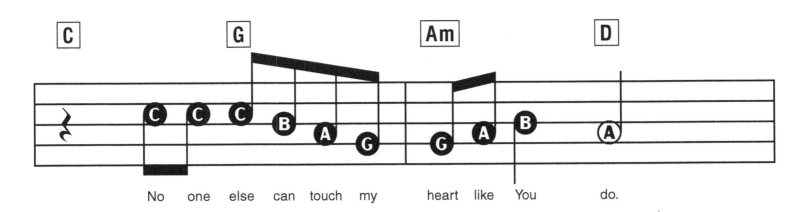

No one else can touch my heart like You do.

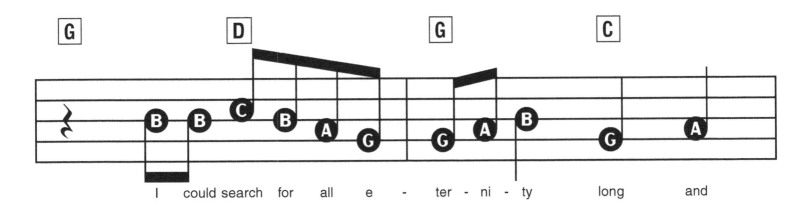

I could search for all e - ter - ni - ty long and

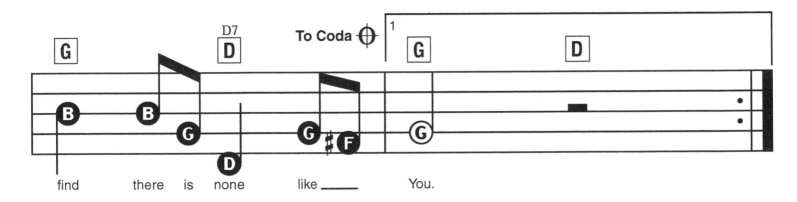

find there is none like ____ You.

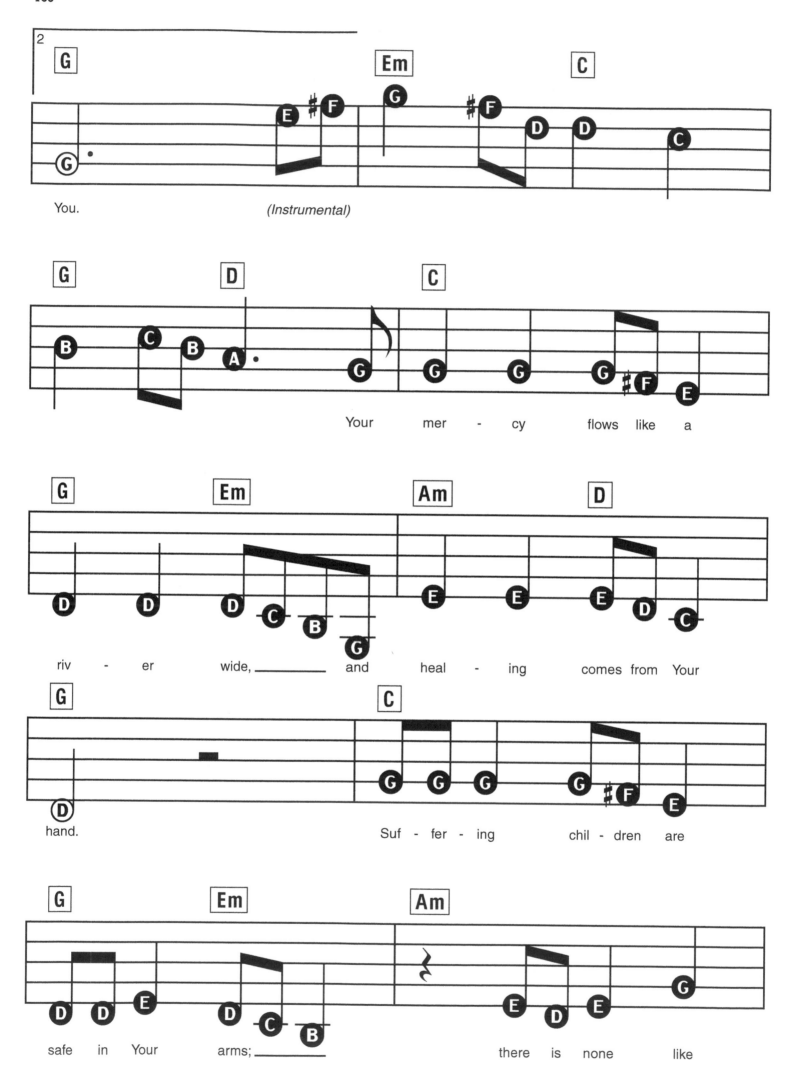

137

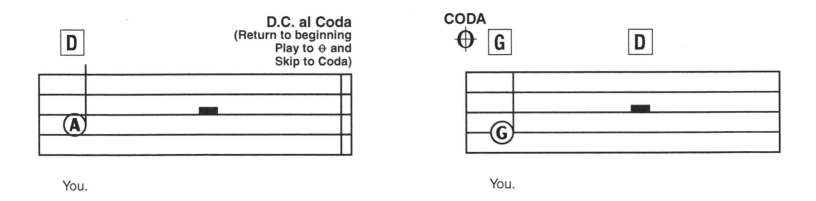

You.

You.

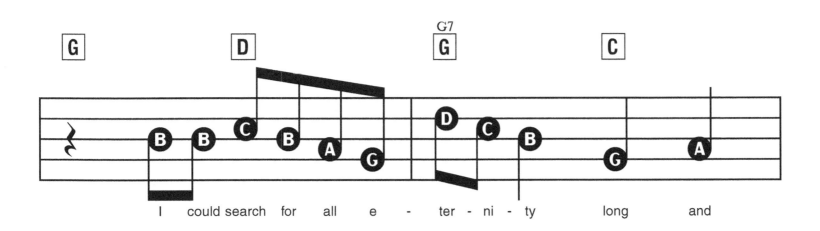

I could search for all e - ter - ni - ty long and

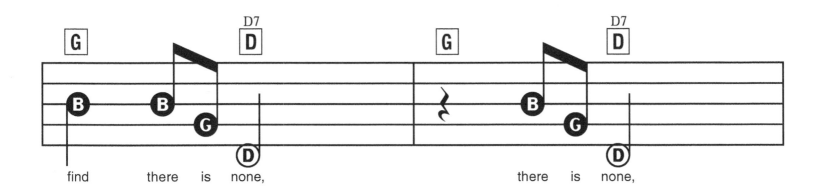

find there is none, there is none,

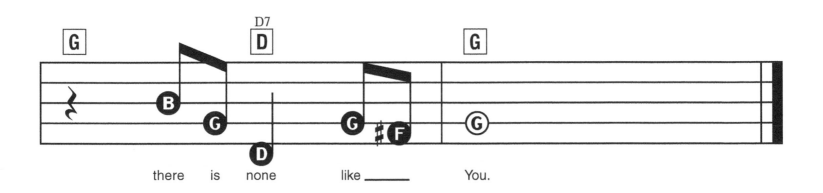

there is none like _____ You.

Take My Life
(Holiness)

Registration 8
Rhythm: Ballad or 8 Beat

Words and Music by
Scott Underwood

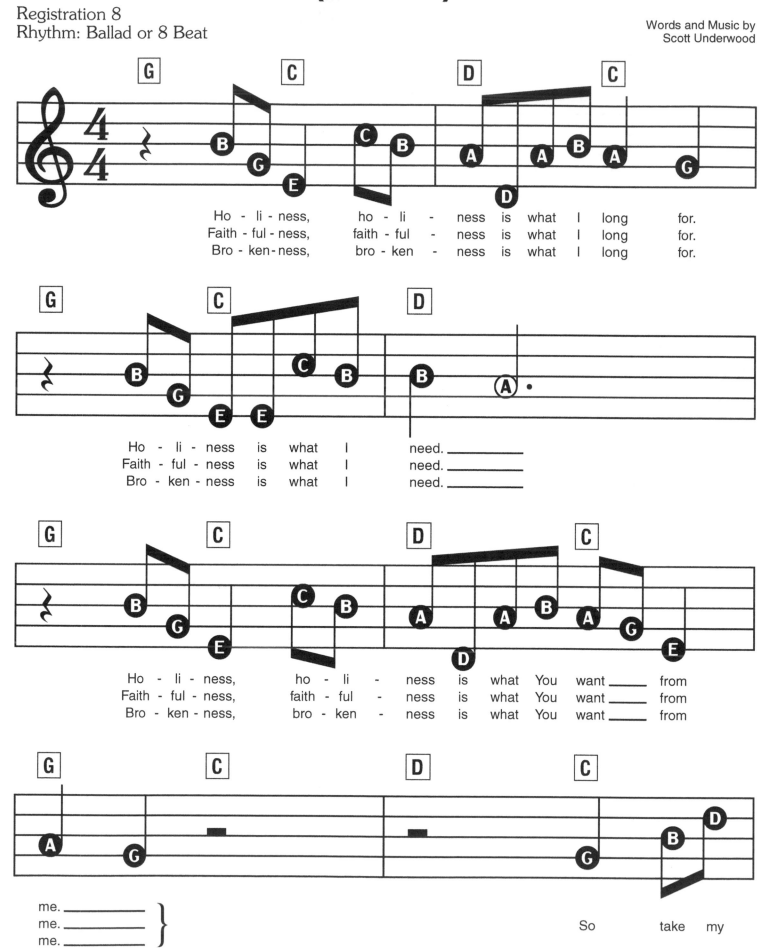

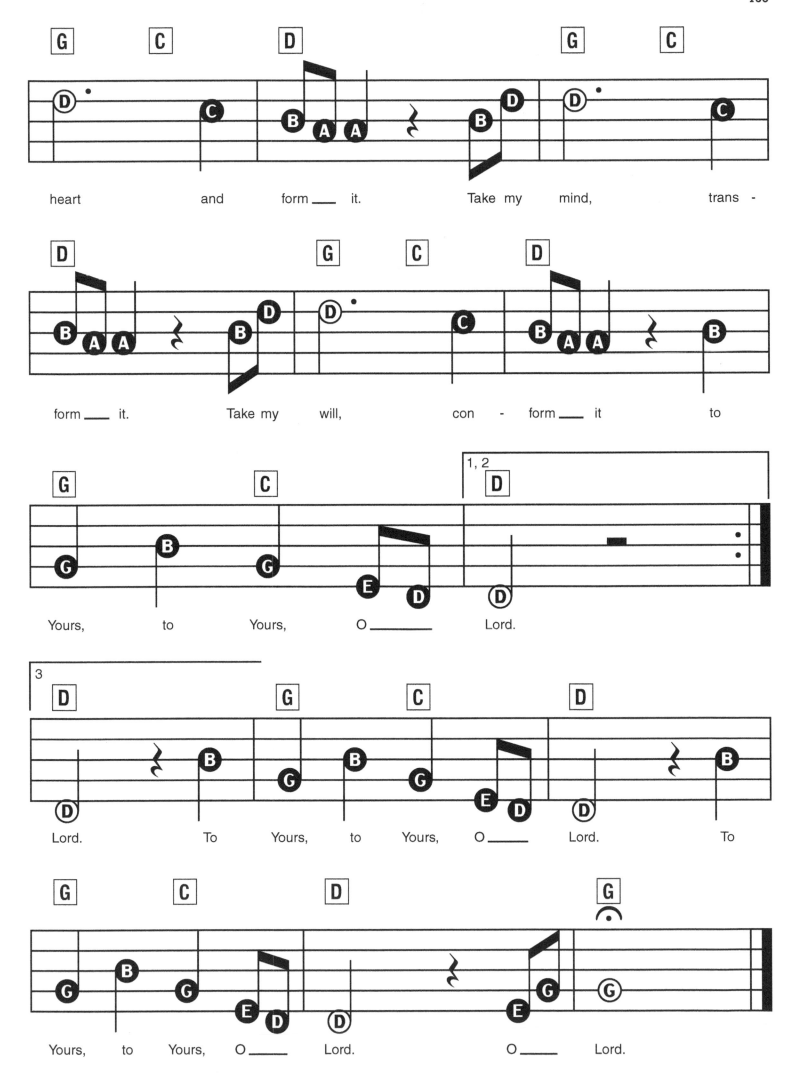

There Is a Redeemer

Registration 8
Rhythm: Ballad

Words and Music by
Melody Green

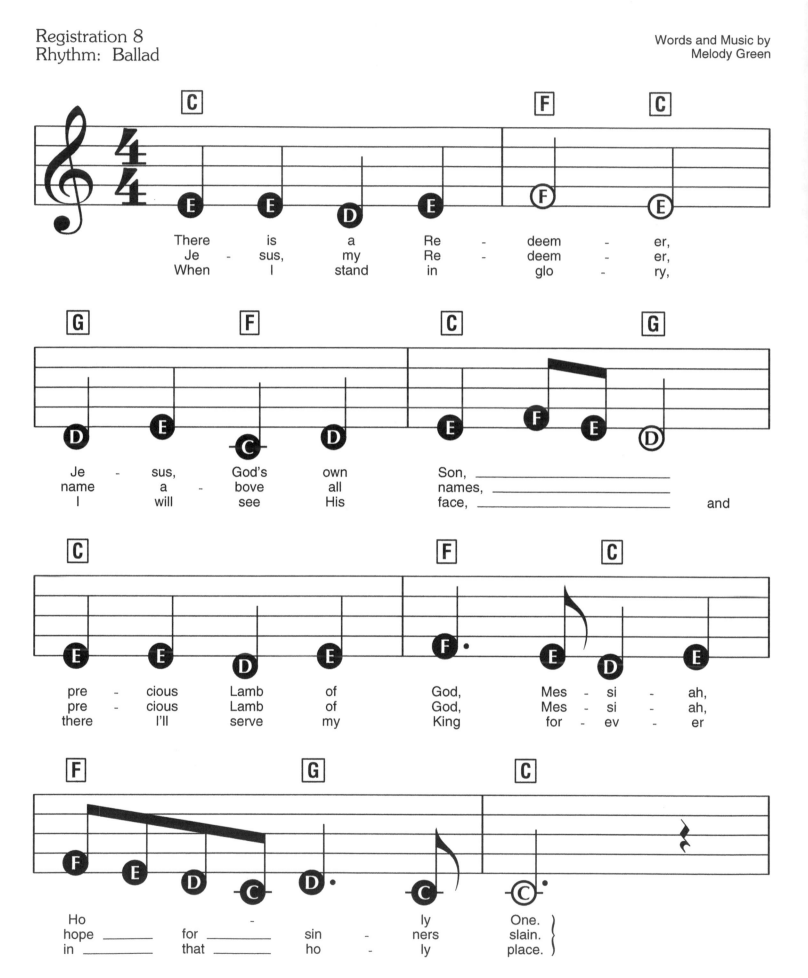

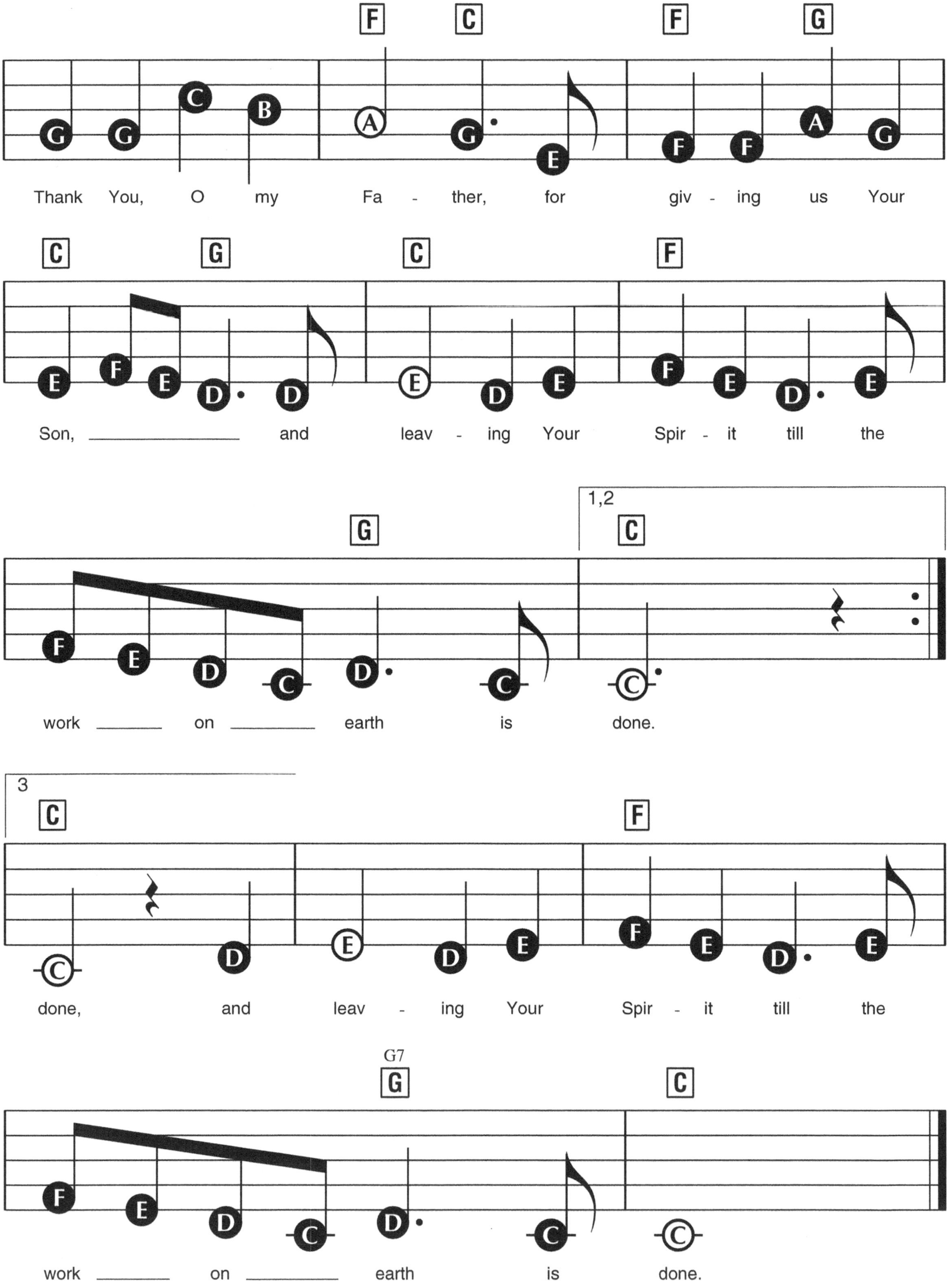
F C F G
Thank You, O my Fa - ther, for giv - ing us Your
C G C F
Son, and leav - ing Your Spir - it till the
G
1,2
C
work on earth is done.
3
C F
done, and leav - ing Your Spir - it till the
G7
G C
work on earth is done.

This Is the Day

Registration 5
Rhythm: Fox Trot

Words and Music by
Les Garrett

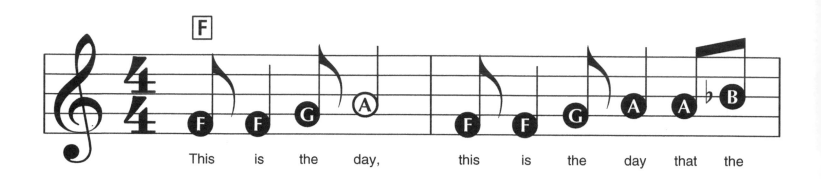

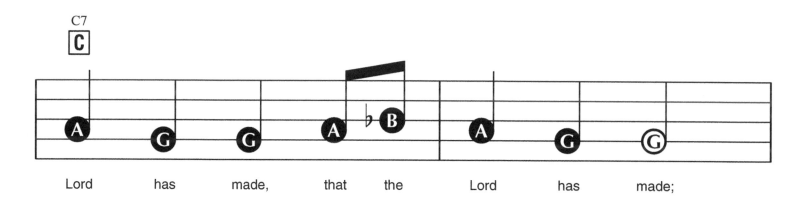

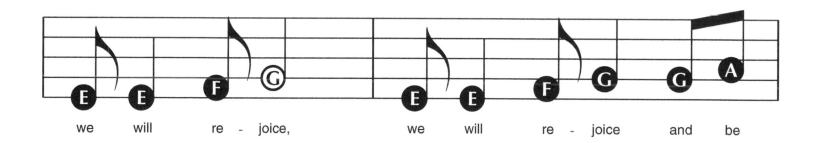

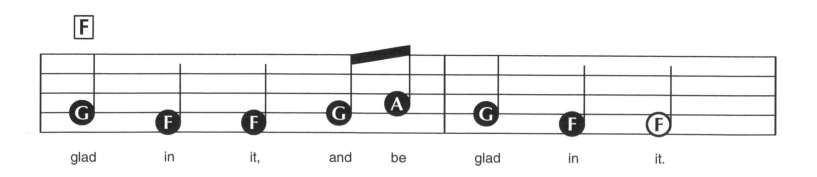

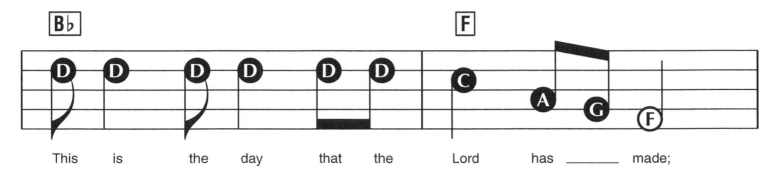

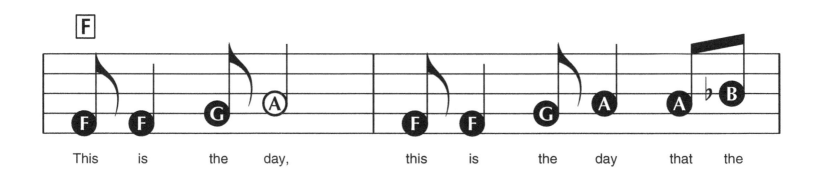

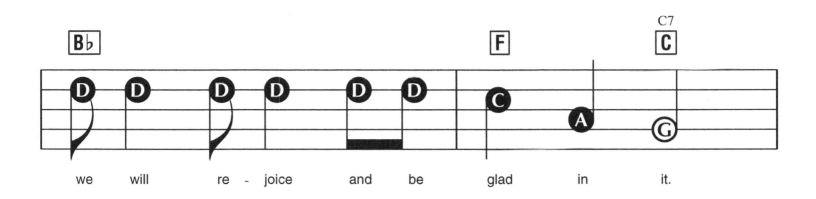

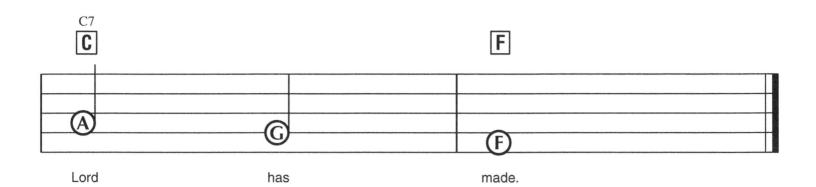

Thy Word

Registration 1
Rhythm: Ballad

Words and Music by Michael W. Smith
and Amy Grant

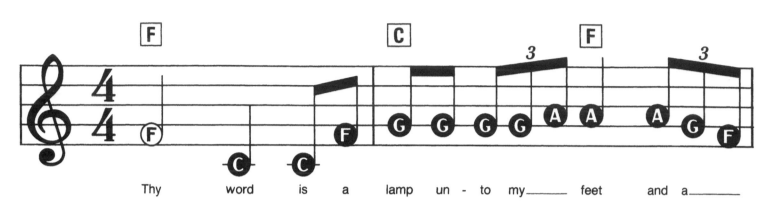

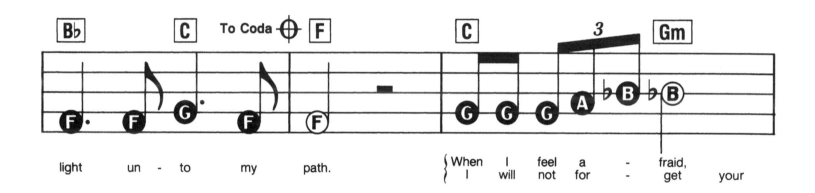

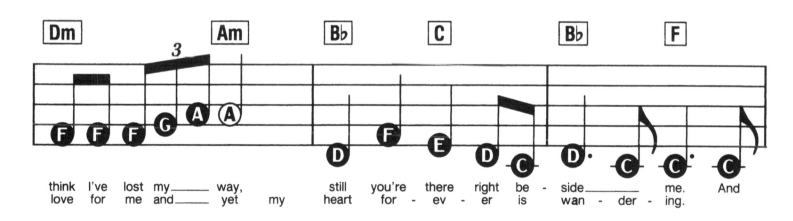

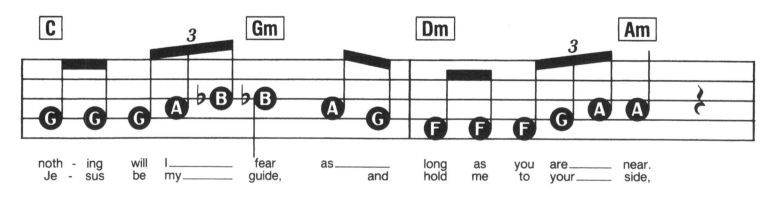

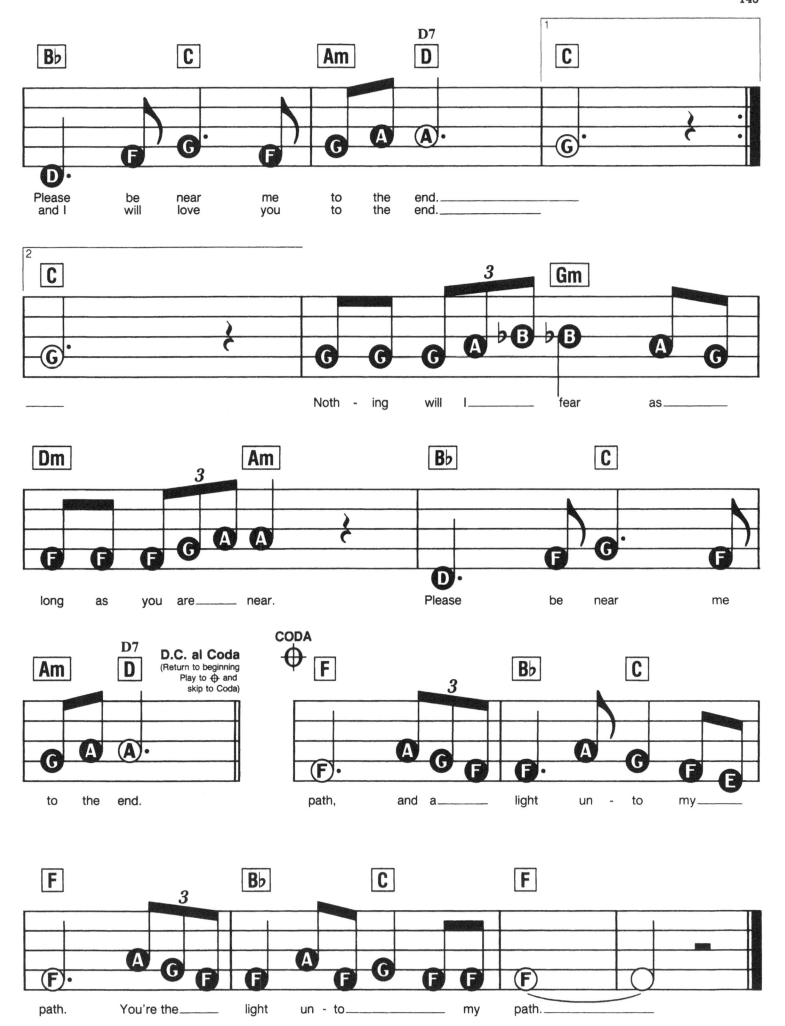

We Bow Down

Registration 8
Rhythm: Waltz

Words and Music by
Twila Paris

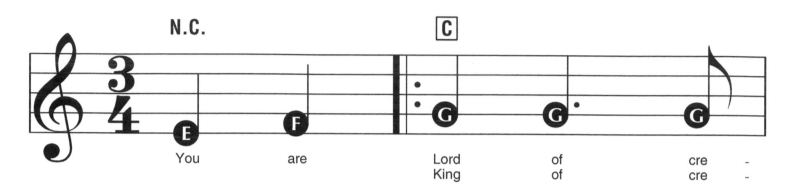

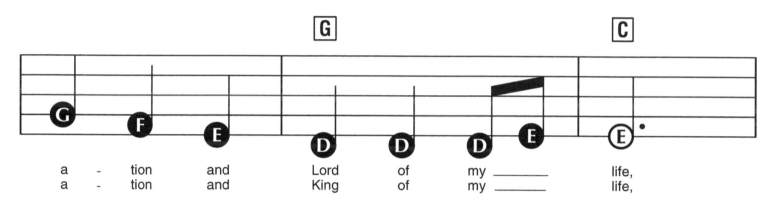

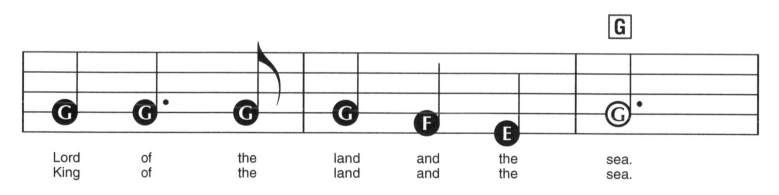

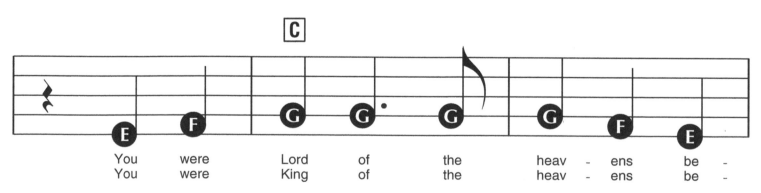

147

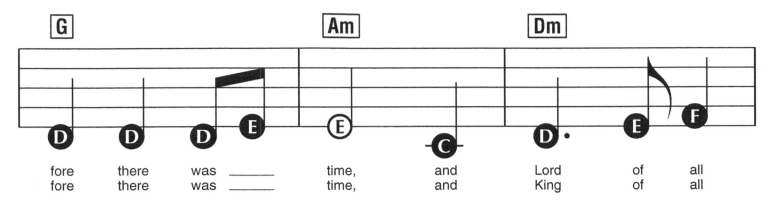

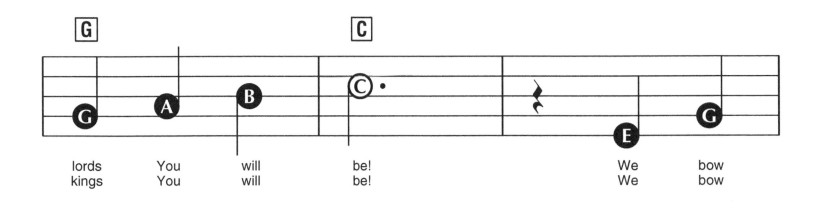

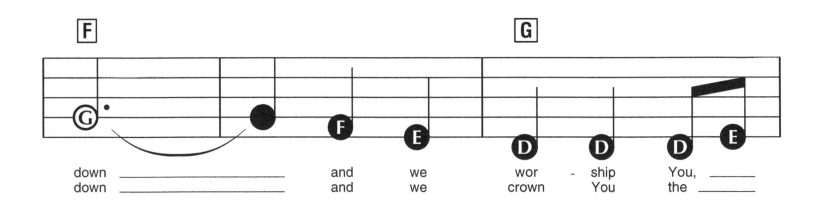

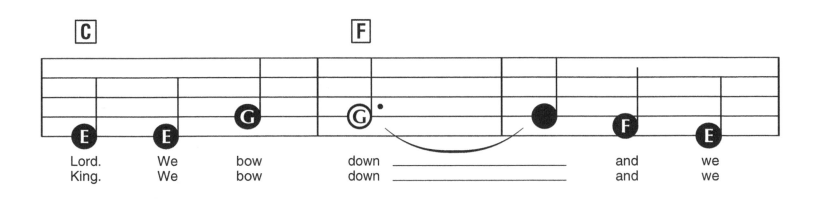

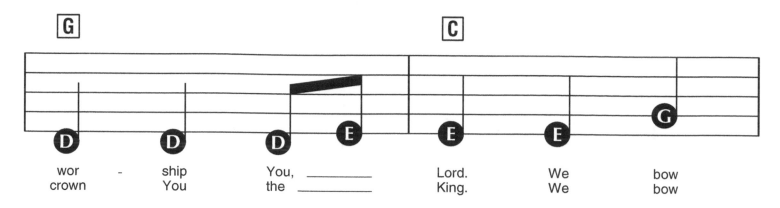

wor - ship You, _____ Lord. We bow
crown You the _____ King. We bow

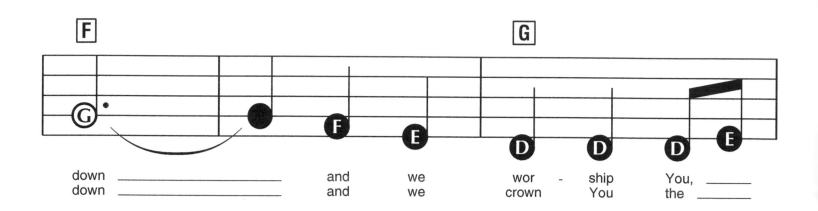

down _____ and we
down _____ and we

wor - ship You, _____
crown You the _____

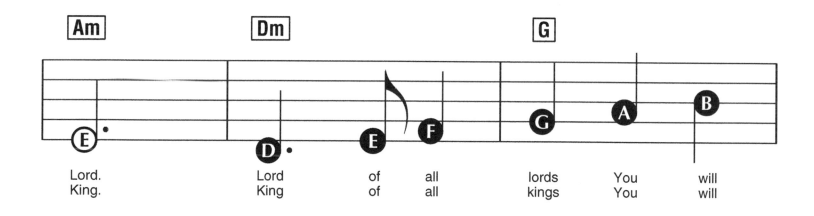

Lord. Lord of all lords You will
King. King of all kings You will

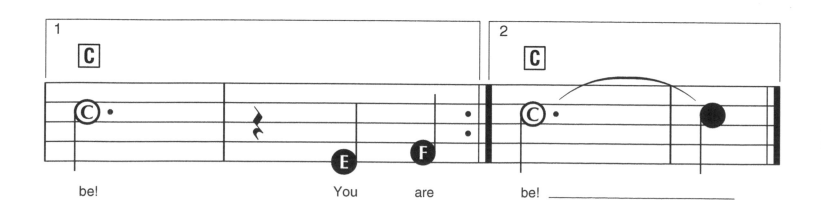

be! You are
be! _____

We Fall Down

Registration 8
Rhythm: Ballad

Words and Music by
Chris Tomlin

We fall down, we lay our crowns at the feet of Je - sus, the great - ness of mer - cy and love at the feet of Je - sus. And we cry, "Ho - ly, ho - ly, ho - ly," and we cry, "Ho - ly, ho - ly, ho - ly," and we cry, "Ho - ly, ho - ly, ho - ly is the Lamb." _____

We Will Glorify

Registration 1
Rhythm: Waltz

Words and Music by
Twila Paris

We will glo - ri - fy the King of kings, we will
ho - vah reigns in maj - es - ty, we will

glo - ri - fy the _____ Lamb; we will
bow be - fore His _____ throne; we will

glo - ri - fy the
wor - ship Him in

Lord of lords, who _____ is the great I _____ Am. Lord Je -
right - eous - ness, we will wor - ship Him a -

lone.

He is

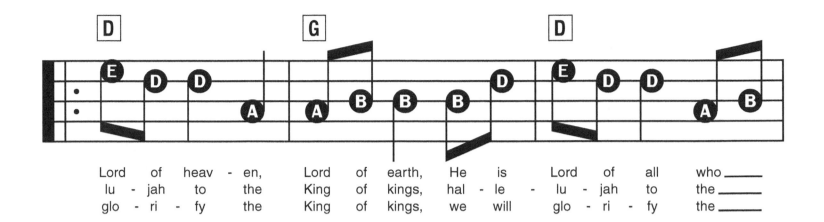

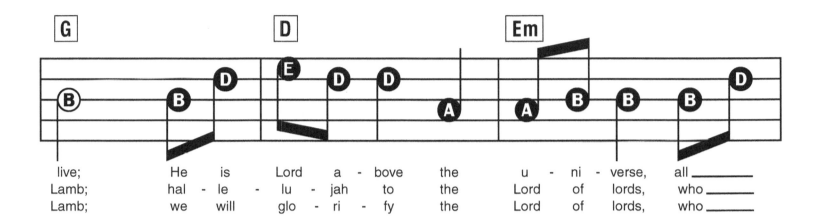

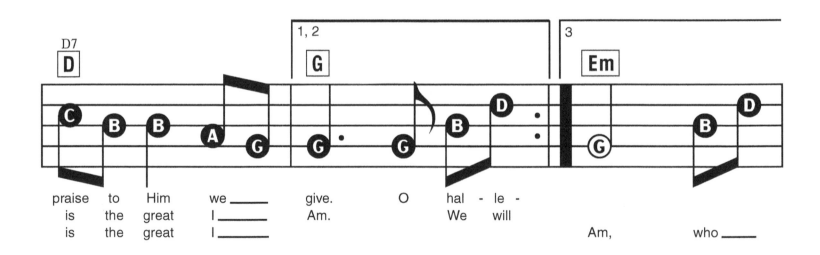

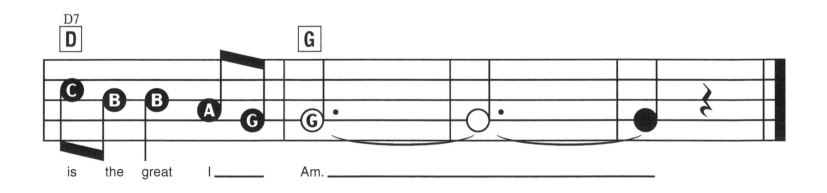

Worthy Is the Lamb

Registration 8
Rhythm: Ballad or 8 Beat

Words and Music by
Darlene Zschech

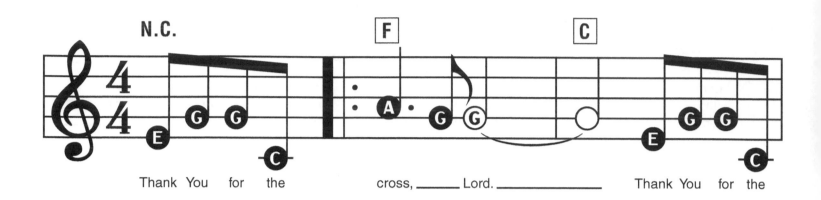

Thank You for the cross, _____ Lord. _____ Thank You for the

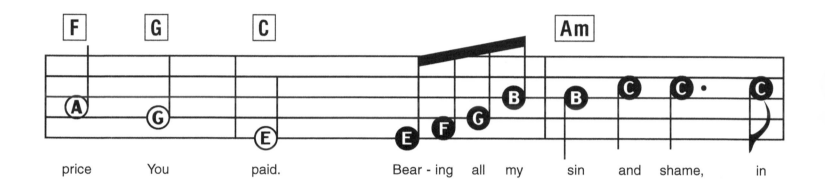

price You paid. Bear - ing all my sin and shame, in

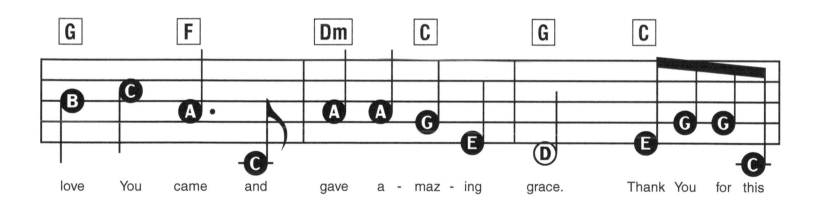

love You came and gave a - maz - ing grace. Thank You for this

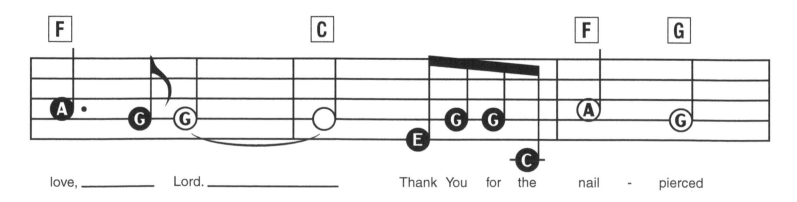

love, _____ Lord. _____ Thank You for the nail - pierced

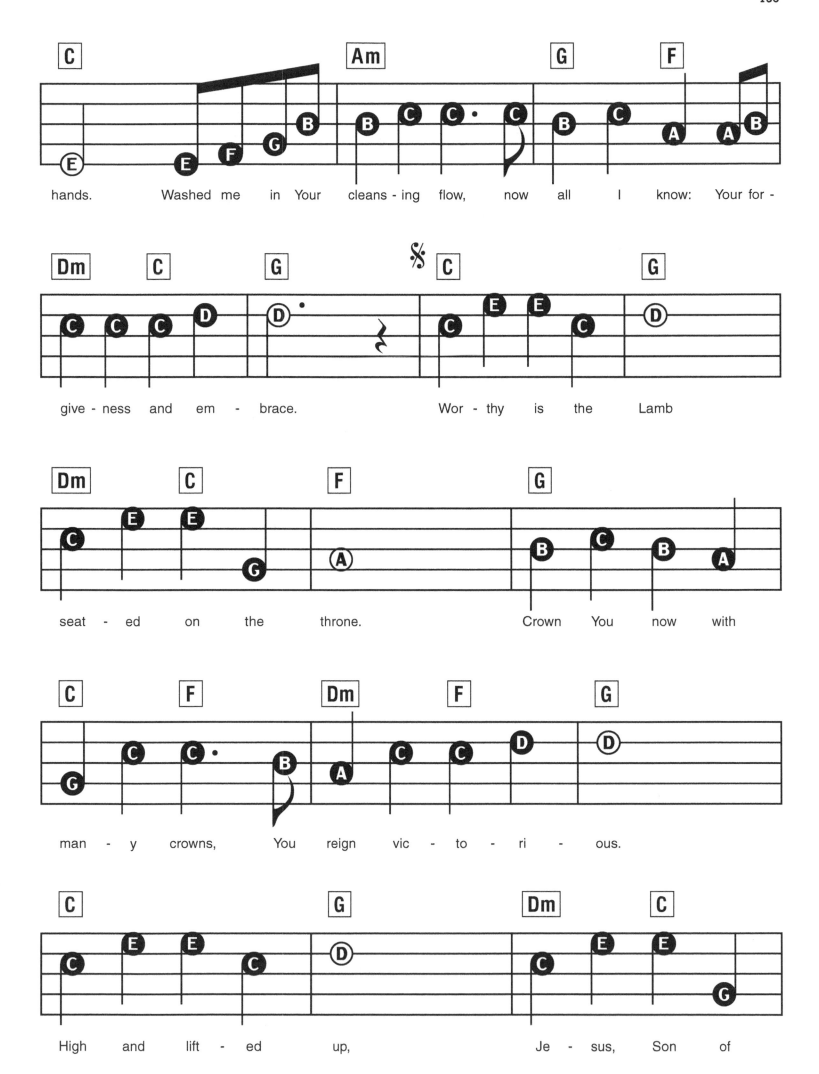

154

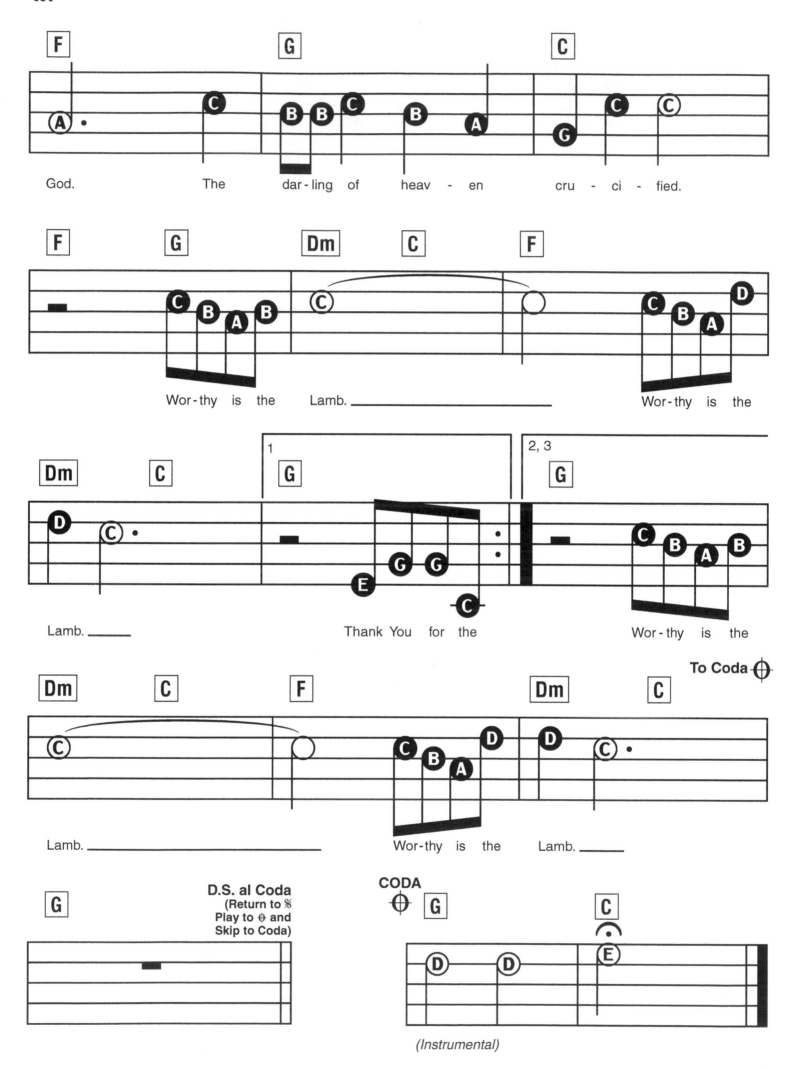

(Instrumental)

You Are My King
(Amazing Love)

Registration 8
Rhythm: Ballad

Words and Music by
Billy James Foote

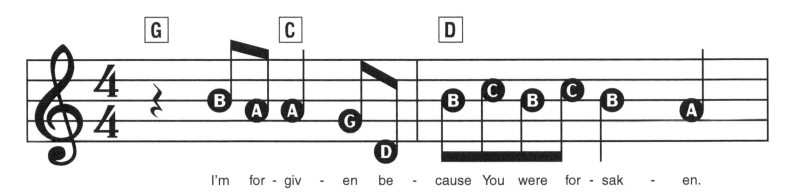

I'm for - giv - en be - cause You were for - sak - en.

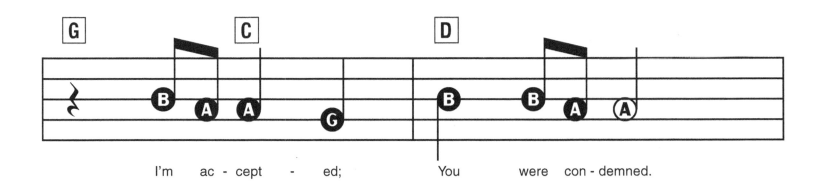

I'm ac - cept - ed; You were con - demned.

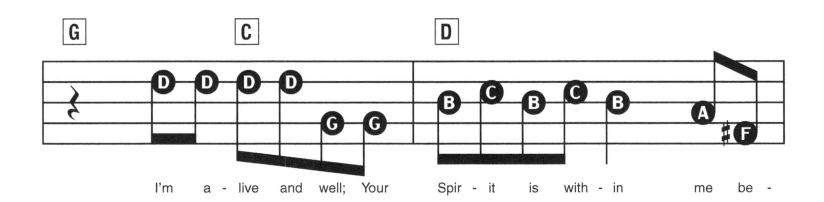

I'm a - live and well; Your Spir - it is with - in me be -

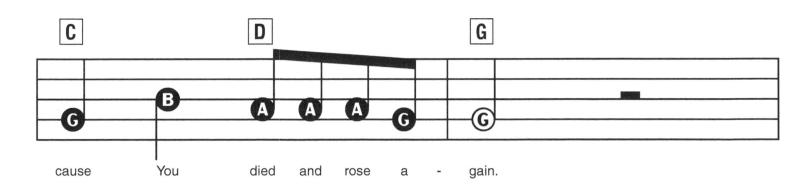

cause You died and rose a - gain.

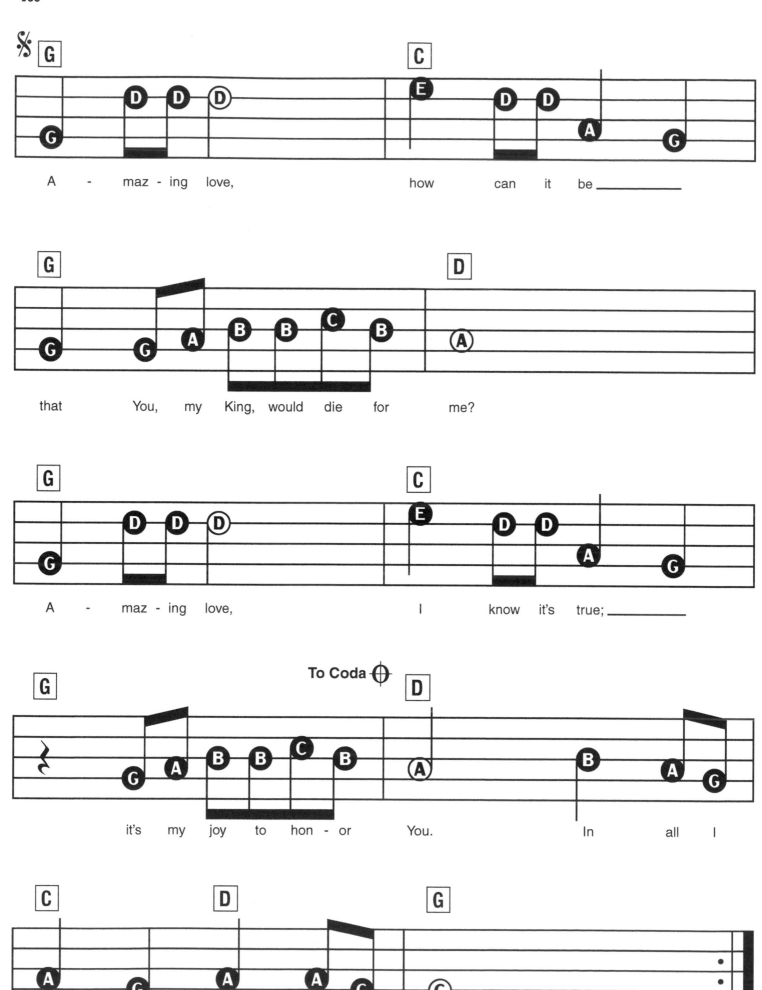

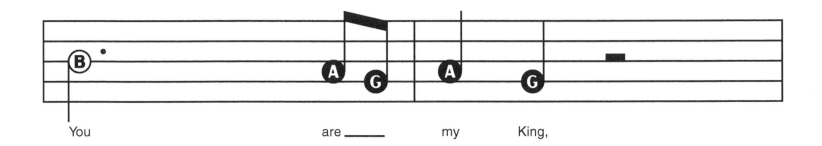

You are ___ my King,

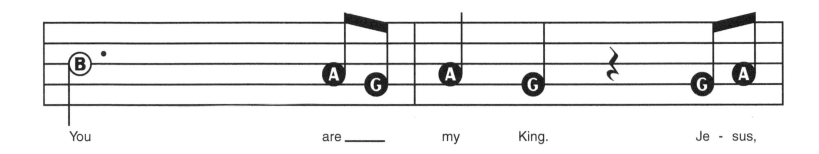

You are ___ my King. Je - sus,

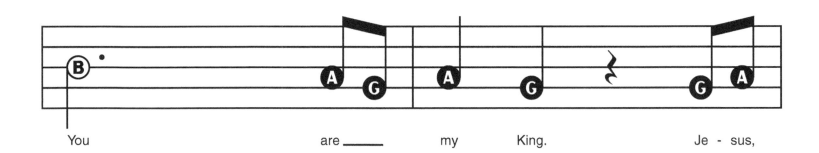

You are ___ my King. Je - sus,

D.S. al Coda
(Return to 𝄋
Play to ⊕ and
Skip to Coda)

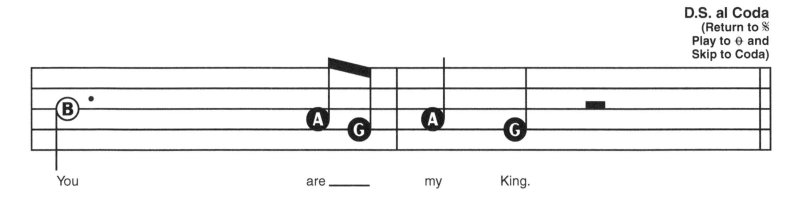

You are ___ my King.

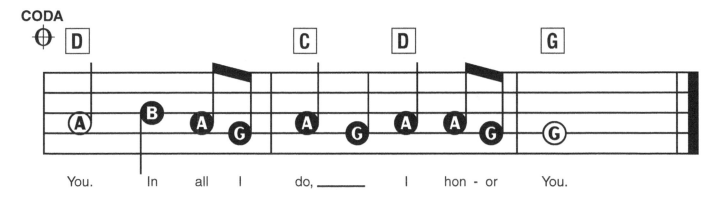

You. In all I do, ___ I hon - or You.

Worthy, You Are Worthy

Registration 1
Rhythm: Ballad

Words and Music by
Don Moen

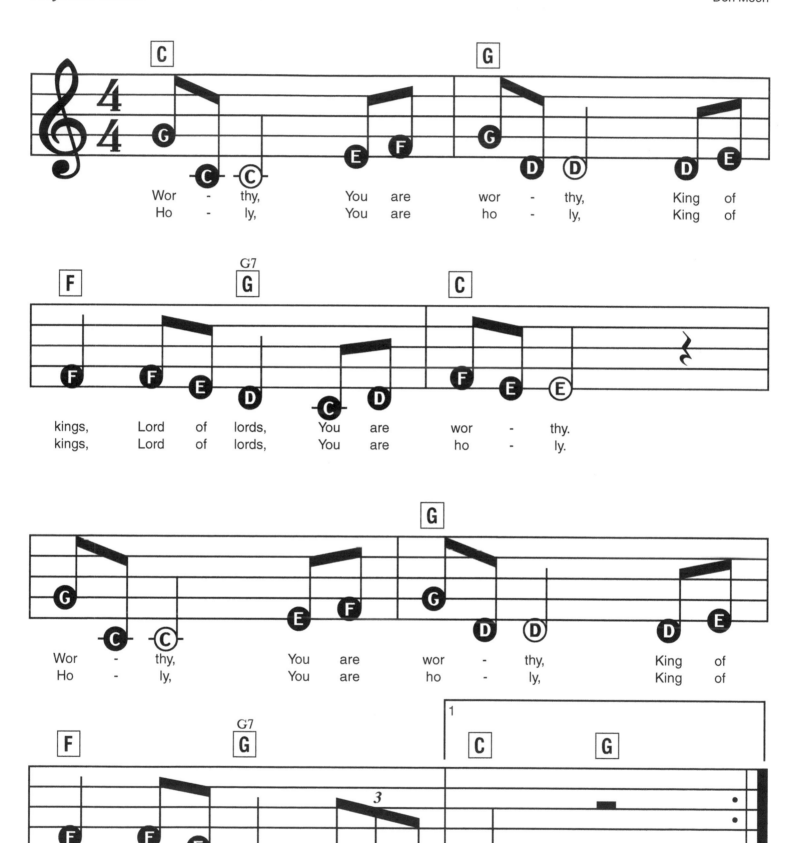

Wor - thy, You are wor - thy, King of
Ho - ly, You are ho - ly, King of

kings, Lord of lords, You are wor - thy.
kings, Lord of lords, You are ho - ly.

Wor - thy, You are wor - thy, King of
Ho - ly, You are ho - ly, King of

kings, Lord of lords, I wor - ship You.
kings, Lord of lords, I wor - ship

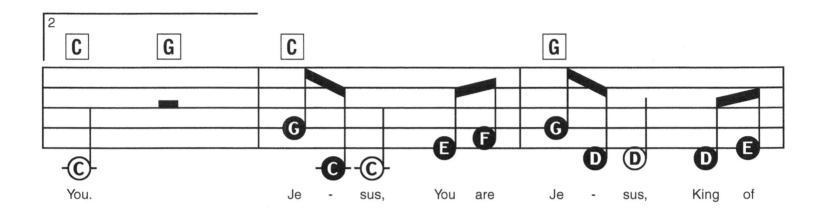

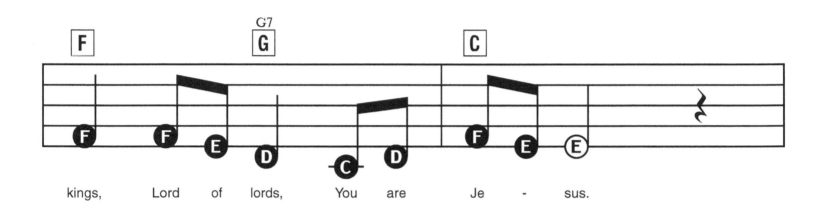

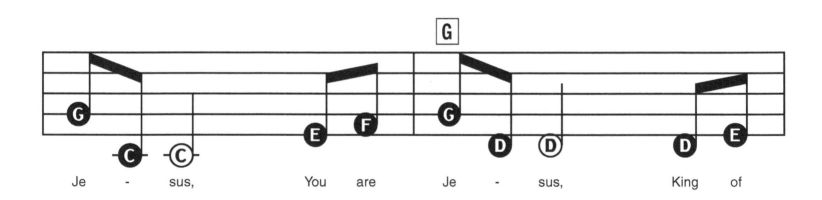

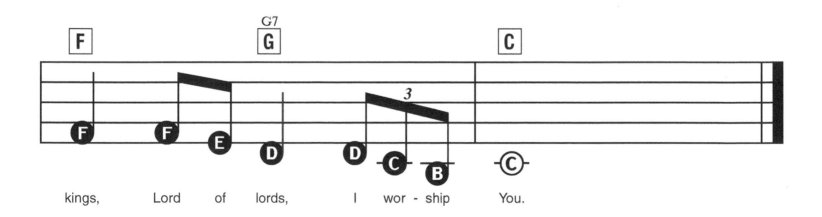

Registration Guide

- Match the Registration number on the song to the corresponding numbered category below. Select and activate an instrumental sound available on your instrument.

- Choose an automatic rhythm appropriate to the mood and style of the song. (Consult your Owner's Guide for proper operation of automatic rhythm features.)

- Adjust the tempo and volume controls to comfortable settings.

Registration

1	Mellow	Flutes, Clarinet, Oboe, Flugel Horn, Trombone, French Horn, Organ Flutes
2	Ensemble	Brass Section, Sax Section, Wind Ensemble, Full Organ, Theater Organ
3	Strings	Violin, Viola, Cello, Fiddle, String Ensemble, Pizzicato, Organ Strings
4	Guitars	Acoustic/Electric Guitars, Banjo, Mandolin, Dulcimer, Ukulele, Hawaiian Guitar
5	Mallets	Vibraphone, Marimba, Xylophone, Steel Drums, Bells, Celesta, Chimes
6	Liturgical	Pipe Organ, Hand Bells, Vocal Ensemble, Choir, Organ Flutes
7	Bright	Saxophones, Trumpet, Mute Trumpet, Synth Leads, Jazz/Gospel Organs
8	Piano	Piano, Electric Piano, Honky Tonk Piano, Harpsichord, Clavi
9	Novelty	Melodic Percussion, Wah Trumpet, Synth, Whistle, Kazoo, Perc. Organ
10	Bellows	Accordion, French Accordion, Mussette, Harmonica, Pump Organ, Bagpipes